About the Author

Siobhan is an award-winning author, blogger, editorial consultant and coach. She loves daring others to love, create and dream and show their true face to the world.

You can find her online at:

Website: **www.daretodreamcoaching.co.uk**

Twitter: **@SiobhanCurham**

Facebook: **Siobhan Curham Author**

Also by Siobhan Curham

NON-FICTION

Antenatal & Postnatal Depression

Finding Your Inner Cherokee

True Face

FICTION

The Sweet Revenge of the Football Widows

True Love Always

The Scene Stealers

Dear Dylan

Finding Cherokee Brown

Shipwrecked

Dark of the Moon

The Moonlight Dreamers

Praise for Siobhan's Non-Fiction

DARE TO DREAM
'A true writer, exploring the heartfelt emotions that so often accompany love. Check out "Dare to Love and Lose" to learn what love is really about.' **DatingAdvice.com**

TRUE FACE
'Curham is a lovely writer, who can make the obvious feel fresh and the negative manageable.' **The Debrief**

'An important and inspirational book.' **The Bookseller**

'A rousing and informative read.' **Mumsnet**

'This book is so significant … it made me realise that I was doing things I didn't realise and it's empowered me a lot from a simple read.' **To Another World**

'A great piece of literary inspiration in a world that is often filled with fake voices that can cloud your judgement.' **Sister Spooky**

'It feels like you have a wise sister talking to you … True Face is inspirational.' **Luna's Little Library**

'A brilliant concept … I felt like a more confident, more honest version of myself once I'd finished.' **Teen Book Hoots**

'I felt much more inspired after finishing True Face. So much so that I stopped to write a letter to myself, reminding myself of how far I've come, despite the obstacles that have been in my way.' **Chrissi Reads**

'Offers some really good tips and advice for helping you come to terms with who you are and get to grips with the issues that affect you … A great book.' **The Big Book Project**

FINDING YOUR INNER CHEROKEE

'*Finding Your Inner Cherokee is a very empowering and inspiring book … it helps you develop vital self-knowledge and inner strength, which will serve you well over a life-time.*' **Claude Knights, CEO, Kidscape.**

'*An outstanding guide that stands out from the market entirely. I can't recommend this book enough.*' **Books and Writers JNR**

'*Read this book, because not only will you know yourself better than you did before, but you will put it down with a new sense of confidence and self-assurance.*' **A Day-Dreamer's World**

'*It feels like a trusted friend is talking you through ways to cope with the struggles you're facing.*' **Hannah's Haven**

'*What a lovely, hopeful and inspiring book Finding Your Inner Cherokee is.*' **Fluttering Butterflies**

'*Completely empowering … the concept is pure gold.*' **Daisy Chain Book Reviews**

DARE TO DREAM

Inspirational musings on

Life, Love & Creativity

Siobhan Curham

Dare to Dream
Published 2015 by Dare to Dream

Printed by CreateSpace

Copyright © 2015 Siobhan Curham
The moral rights of the author have been asserted

ISBN 978-0-9927464-6-9

www.siobhancurham.co.uk
www.daretodreamcoaching.co.uk

Cover design by Michael A. Hill

In memory of Michelle Richards

...one of the most inspirational, fearless dreamers I've ever been lucky enough to know.

£1 from every sale of Dare to Dream will be donated to Michelle's favourite charity, Leuka, helping find a cure for leukaemia.

Contents

Part Two: Love

Part Three: Creativity

Introduction

In February 2013 I started a blog called *Dare to Dream*. I had no great worldly ambitions for this blog - I didn't even invest in a proper domain name, so it ended up with the rather unwieldy address: **daretodreamcoaching.blogspot.co.uk** which I imagine, in the world of websites, is a bit like being clad in a hulking suit of armour, clomping around self-consciously amongst the sleek and shiny dotcoms.

In the ten years prior to starting the blog, life had taken me on an entire theme park's worth of roller coaster rides. I'd left a marriage, landed a publishing deal, had four books published, lost a publishing deal, thought my life was over, started running weekly writers' workshops ... and realised that an exciting new life had only just begun, got diagnosed with an auto-immune disease which (until the meds kicked in) made me cry over *every*thing - like running out of peanut butter when all the shops were closed (oh, the agony!), trained as a life coach, fell in love, self-published a novel, almost lost my partner to cancer, home-schooled my son, went through a soul-destroying break-up, realised my son and I needed a fresh start so stuck a pin in a map (or the online equivalent, hovering a cursor over Google maps) and moved to a town we'd never been to before (best move ever), won a national book award (for the self-published novel), landed new publishing deals in the UK, France and Germany, trained to become a dance teacher purely to satisfy my long term *Kids from Fame* fantasy, and embarked upon a quest to find true love, which turned into a quest to find God or the Universe or whatever you want to call the *something more* we all experience when we allow ourselves to be truly silent and still.

As a result, I was brimming over with things I wanted to write about life and love and creativity. Starting a blog seemed like the natural thing to do but without the guise of fiction to hide behind I was really self-conscious about writing so personally, so I kept it very low key.

Every week or so, I'd post a musing and politely mention it in passing to my Facebook friends and after a while I noticed that they were sharing it with their friends and I had actual strangers commenting and liking posts - a weird and wonderful feeling.

Then one day, a website based in California called DatingAdvice.com got in touch to tell me they'd awarded *Dare to Dream* a place in their **Top Ten Blogs for Dating Courage**. My first instinct was to ask, *'but how the heck did you even know it existed?!'* They made special mention of a post I'd written about a relationship break-up I'd been through. It was probably the most personal thing I'd ever written, so I was deeply touched by this recognition.

More and more people started emailing me about the blog and how it had resonated with them. They opened up to me about their own lives and struggles. Here's an extract from an email that touched me so much it made me cry (and not in an auto-immune-disease-running-out-of-peanut-butter way):

'As I read your posts, I just get this sense that everything will be okay. That no matter what path my life will take, I'll survive … perhaps prosper. You just seem so detached from expected social norms. You do what you want, you take risks, you rise above challenges. I can't tell you how comforting it is to see you succeed, but also to see you fail and carry on. I feel as if I have a chance. That, with grit and poetry, I might just find a way to write my own books and share them with the world. That I can write … and be happy.'

I love the way the writer of the email talks about 'grit and poetry' – isn't that what we all need to get us through this crazy ride called life?

Grit and poetry.

This year, I decided to relaunch my coaching practice, having put it on the back-burner for the past three years to focus on my writing. *Dare to Dream* has been given a much-needed make-over - and a sleaker domain name: **daretodreamcoaching.co.uk** - please call by and have a browse around. And I couldn't think of a better way to mark the occasion than by publishing *Dare to Dream*, the book.

This book is a collection of some of the most popular posts from the blog, plus over 100 pages of brand-spanking new and previously unpublished material.

It covers everything from daring to love and lose, to how to write a book in a month, to the truth about meditation (*contrary to popular belief, it's not about sitting for hours in a knee-breaking lotus pose with a mind completely void of thoughts*) to navigating the dating world, falling wildly in love with your work, dancing yourself happy, and how to cure constipation - *creative* constipation.

I hope you enjoy it and I hope it leaves you raring - and daring - to dream.

Siobhan x

Part One: Life

"I went to the woods because I wished to live deliberately, to front only the essential facts of life, see if I could not learn what it had to teach, and not, when I came to die, discover that I had not lived."

Henry David Thoreau

Everything Changes When You Dare to Dream

When I was a child my parents didn't have a TV. Not even a portable.

This tragic fact meant that I either died of boredom or I learnt to love books.

So I learnt to love books.

And, a few years into my love affair, I started to dream of one day becoming a writer.

I can remember gazing at the bookshelf in my bedroom and thinking how amazing it would be to have actually written a shelf-full of books of my own.

Fast forward a few more years and I had a place at uni, studying English Literature and Film.

But two years into my course, as described in gory detail elsewhere in this book, I lost my confidence, dropped out of uni, gave up on my dream and ended up working in the complaints department for a frozen food company.

Suddenly, all I was writing were grovelling letters apologising for the dead insects people had found in their ice-cream.

It wasn't great.

Especially when irate customers actually *sent* me the dead critters they'd found, cellotaped spread-eagled to the page in all their creepy-crawly glory.

One thing I discovered during that time is that when you allow your dreams to die, a part of you dies too.

My life became a hamster wheel of working Monday to Friday, and clubbing, drinking and drugging at the weekends.

Although everything seemed fun and carefree on the surface, inside I felt like a big fat failure.

I was a university drop-out, in a job I hated, and the only time I ever felt any kind of joy - blitzed on a dance floor - I was painfully aware that it was only ever an artificial high.

Then one day, I read an article about achieving your dream life.

One of the exercises it recommended was to write about your perfect day.

You had to forget all about your doubts and fears and just write a stream of consciousness about what a perfect day in your perfect life would look and feel like.

- *Where would you be living?*

- *Who would you be with?*

- *What work would you be doing?*

- *How would you look?*

- *How would you feel?*

- *What would you be doing for fun?*

- *Who would you see?*

Although slightly cynical, I decided to give it a go and as soon as I started writing, something weird happened.

I managed to silence all the negative crap my inner voice of doom used to taunt me with and loads of positive dreams and images flowed from my pen.

At the time, I was living in a flat above a chip shop in London.

I wrote about an idyllic life in the country, living in a cottage where I wasn't plagued by nightmares of deep-fat-fryers catching fire and killing me in my sleep.

Then, emboldened by this new-found positivity, my old writing dreams sparked back into life.

Despite being a university drop-out trapped in frozen-food-hell, I wrote in glorious detail about my dream life as a published author with a shelf full of books of my own.

And after that, everything changed.

Writing in such vivid detail had given me a real taster of my dream life.

And giving myself permission to dare to dream triggered a fundamental change in me.

Now, instead of blocking my dreams, I actively looked for ways in which I could make that amazing perfect day become a reality.

It was another three years before my first book was published, but that first exercise played such a crucial first step.

I now live in a cottage two whole streets away from my nearest chip shop - close enough for takeaway but not close enough to perish in a fat-fryer inferno - perfect!

This is my thirteenth book.

My shelf of dreams has finally become a reality.

And the pursuit of this dream has led to some of the happiest and most fulfilling moments of my life.
So if fear and lack of confidence currently have you in a choke-hold, make some time to do the Perfect Day exercise yourself.

Make sure that you won't be interrupted - for this exercise to work you really need to get into your flow.

Make a pact with yourself before you begin to abandon all doubt and fear for the duration of the exercise.

Don't get hung up on spelling or grammar.

Just write, write, write, using all of the senses in your description so that it really comes alive.

And allow your dreams to fly free.

Everything Changes When You Dare to Dream ... Part Two

"All people dream, but not equally. Those who dream by night in the dusty recesses of their mind, wake in the morning to find that it was vanity. But the dreamers of the day are dangerous people, for they dream their dreams with open eyes, and make them come true."
D H Lawrence

I love the quote by D H Lawrence above - when you dream your dreams with open eyes; when you put them at the heart of your waking life and use them as a compass to guide you forward, they have an uncanny knack of coming true.
But of course, none of this is possible if you are under the influence of fear. So, on that spine-chilling note...

There are many exercises designed to help you conquer fear. Here's one of my favourites:

Flush Off, Fear!

Write a list of all the fears holding you back from achieving your dreams. Fears that you aren't good enough / young enough / old enough / attractive enough / clever enough / *enough* enough. Write them all down and don't let any escape your gaze. Fears can be crafty buggers and you don't want any popping up later to catch you off guard. Then carry your list through to the bathroom. That's right - the bathroom. In suitably dramatic fashion, tear it up into tiny pieces and flush it down the toilet whilst chanting, *'Flush off, fear'** repeatedly until every last one of them has gone. (**Please note: You don't have to do the chanting bit if anyone else is in the house at the time.*) Then return to your notepad and write another list – this time of all the things you are proud of achieving in your life. These can be achievements in any area of your life, from career to family and friends, to personal. Now, if you're British, I know you'd rather stick your tongue in the sandwich toaster than admit to being proud of anything, so for the purposes of this exercise, try pretending that you're American. And reassure yourself that nobody is ever going to see your list, *ever*, so you can really go for it.

Once you've written your list, think back to those fears of yours now languishing in a pipe somewhere and see if you can use your list of achievements to counter them. Let me give you an example from a coaching client I once did this exercise with:

My client's dream was to be a writer but she was too scared to send her book to an agent. When we went through her list of achievements it turned out that she had come to the UK from India as a young woman, not knowing anyone over here and not able to speak a word of English. And yet within a year she had a new circle of friends, could speak the language fluently and was loving her new life. I held this incredible achievement up to her and then asked why on earth a woman who was capable of such breath-taking courage and chutzpah was terrified at the mere thought of mailing a manuscript! She started laughing her head off and I could see her fear dissolving right before my eyes. And now, several years later, she is the published author of three books - internationally. Take heed, dear reader - and get flushing!

Dream Board

Once you've dealt with your fears, it's time to get really clear on exactly what your dreams are. Along with the *Perfect Day* exercise, one of the simplest and most fun ways to do this is by creating a dream board. A dream board is basically a board, on which you place images and words that symbolise your dreams. I told you it was simple.

Personally, I love dream boards and I always create one when I'm working on a new book or major new life goal. But I think it's important to clarify something.

They aren't magic.

Just because you stick a picture of Bruce Springsteen on your board it does not mean that you're going to wake up one morning to find him shirtlessly singing *'Born to Run'* to you from the end of your bed. Trust me, I've tried. But what a dream board does do is help create a clear picture of your dream life and imprint it upon your mind. To go back to the D H Lawrence quote; it helps you to dream *with your eyes wide open.* And then, because you are so clear on what it is that you want to achieve, you are way more likely to make the decisions required to manifest your dreams. And that's when it can start to feel magical. You find yourself in just the right places, at just the right time. Or coming across just the right book, or just the right person to help you achieve your goals. It's also a really good excuse to get busy with a Pritt stick and make a fun collage.

Happy cutting and pasting, *Dare to Dreamers*!

Always Remember to Blaze a Trail

2009 was one of the worst years of my life. Or - as the Queen would put it - my annus horribilus.

My then partner had been diagnosed with cancer - a brain tumour - and told he only had months to live.

A close member of my family was being bullied at school and becoming a shadow of their former self before our eyes.

And my writing career felt dead in the water.

There were many times during that year when I felt as if I was drowning. I'm a natural born optimist but there are times when life throws so much crap at you that you just can't see a way through.

I remember one day, after I'd burnt some toast, going back to bed and crying for about an hour.

I'd tried so hard to maintain a strong and bright exterior to the outside world but inside, I could feel myself slipping away.

It's at times like these that you need an intervention. You need someone to step in and shine a light on your darkness.

For me, it came in the form of a conversation with a friend.

It was one of those rich, late night conversations in which you really connect with another human being and the rest of the world and all of your problems temporarily fade away. My friend was a fellow writer and from a similar background, growing up on a London council estate. He *got* me. And I *got* him. He'd seen that I was drowning and so he set about throwing me a life-line made from words - it definitely helped that he was a poet.

Amongst many other things, he told me that he'd always thought of me as being just like a shooting star and that I mustn't ever stop blazing a trail.

For most of that year I'd felt more like one of those dud home fireworks that splutters and fizzles out to disappointed sighs. It felt incomprehensible that he should see me in this way.

But his words lodged in my brain - and gave me a much needed spark of hope.

I went home emboldened.

My partner wasn't going to die.

My family member wasn't going to be bullied any more.

And I was going to write another book - and publish it myself.

As I knew that it would be all too easy for me to slip back into my feelings of depression, I got a shooting star tattooed on my wrist as a constant reminder. And from that moment on, before I said or did anything, I'd think to myself, *what would a person who's just like a shooting star do? How can I blaze a trail?*

My partner ended up defying the doctors and surviving. Sadly, we broke up, but we remain the very best of friends. He has now been free from cancer for over five years.

I helped my family member who was being bullied move to a new school and they are now back to their happy, carefree self, with a wide group of new friends.

The book I wrote and self-published (*Dear Dylan*) went on to win a national award. I couldn't help smiling when I saw that the award itself was star-shaped.

The book then went to auction and the publishers I signed up with said how much they loved my star tattoo - and could they incorporate it into my name on my book covers?

At the launch party for my second novel with that publisher (*Finding Cherokee Brown*) I stood there about to give a reading and I don't think I've ever felt happier.

There was my ex-boyfriend, smiling and cancer-free. There were the posters of the book with the stars designed into my name. There were my closest friends - my rocks during that terrible time. And there were so many other, newer friends, who didn't even know me back in those dark days.

And there I was, about to read from a book I'd written about bullying - inspired by what we'd been through during that dark time.

It was such an important lesson in never giving up, no matter how hard things get.

And, echoing around my head were my friend's words, said to me but just as applicable to you:

'You're just like a shooting star - don't ever stop blazing a trail.'

Silencing Your Inner Voice of Doom

This week I gave a talk to a high school (*new post about how to conquer abject terror, coming soon*). The talk was about how I became a writer - and the obstacles I faced along the way.
A major obstacle I faced is what I like to call my Inner Voice of Doom. Now one thing I've learnt over the years - especially since becoming a life coach - is that we all have this inner voice telling us that we're not good enough, attractive enough, rich enough, talented enough, *enough* enough. The question is - how do we get it to shut up?

During my talk I asked some of the students to come up and act as my Inner Voice of Doom *(there were LOTS of volunteers)*.
I stood at the front of the stage and they formed a ring round me, one by one taunting me with the things I used to say to myself when I dreamt of becoming a writer:

'YOU CAN'T BE A WRITER'

'YOU'RE FROM A COUNCIL ESTATE'

'PEOPLE FROM COUNCIL ESTATES DON'T BECOME WRITERS'

'YOU DON'T HAVE ANY CONTACTS IN THE PUBLISHING WORLD'

'YOU DON'T HAVE ANYTHING INTERESTING TO WRITE ABOUT'

'YOU DON'T HAVE WHAT IT TAKES'

'YOUR WRITING IS CRAP'

Nice, huh?! The worst thing is, back when I was twenty I let this voice talk me into giving up on my dreams and dropping out of university, and I wasted years in jobs I hated.

After I gave my high school talk, I did a series of workshops with the students, getting them to write down the kinds of things their inner voices of doom like to say. Here are some of the most common ones that came up:

'YOU'RE TOO UGLY'

'YOU'RE NOT GOOD ENOUGH'

'YOU'RE GOING TO MAKE A FOOL OF YOURSELF'

'EVERYONE'S GOING TO LAUGH AT YOU'

'YOU'RE SO STUPID'

'YOU'RE GOING TO FAIL'

Okay, let's get real about this. Your Inner Voice of Doom doesn't belong to another person. It's not as if you have a sneery commentator following you round all day, bellowing insults into a loud hailer.

This voice belongs to you!

Which immediately begs the question: Why? Why do this to yourself?

As I said to the students in my talk - there are enough eejits out there ready to put you down due to their own jealousy or insecurity - the last thing you need to do is add to this. So, how do you get your inner critic to shut up?

One way is to imagine that you're talking to your best friend. If your best friend told you about a dream they really wanted to achieve, would you start wetting yourself laughing and say, *'Ha! You can't do that! You're way too crap!'*

I think not. Or at least, I hope not - and if you did say yes to that question, remind me never to invite *you* to tea! But the most effective technique I've found in overcoming my Inner Voice of Doom is the following three step process:

STEP ONE: *Identify it*
Often, we become so used to our Inner Voice of Doom that we don't even realise we're doing it to ourselves. It becomes the soundtrack to our lives - like a sinister form of elevator muzak. So instead of just accepting it, try to become aware of what's happening, the next time your Inner V of D starts kicking off.

STEP TWO: *Shine a Spotlight on it*
By this, I mean really examine what's going on when you start to hear this voice. Although it can sound really mean, actually, like any bully, this voice is coming from a place of fear. When my Inner Voice of Doom told me that I didn't have what it takes to become a writer, it was my own fear of failure speaking. Ironically, it was trying to protect me, in its own fearful way. By seeing your Voice of Doom as fearful it immediately lessens its power.

STEP THREE: *Come up with an alternative*
What if you were to have a supportive inner cheerleader instead of a voice of doom? What would they say?

In my talk, I got some students to play my inner cheerleader, and say all the things I wish I'd said to myself when I'd been doubting my writing abilities and dropped out of uni:

'YOU ARE GOOD ENOUGH'

'WHO CARES IF YOU CAME FROM A COUNCIL ESTATE?'

'GOING THROUGH HARD TIMES GAVE YOU LOADS TO WRITE ABOUT'

'YOU DON'T HAVE TO HAVE CONTACTS TO MAKE IT AS A WRITER'

'YOU HAVE JUST AS MUCH RIGHT TO WRITE AS ANYONE ELSE'

Here's the thing - we don't *have* to talk to ourselves like we're crap. We have the option to be a whole lot nicer. And as I said before, with enough people out there ready to have a dig at us, don't we owe it to ourselves to be more self-supportive? I know that we can instinctively balk at the notion of bigging ourselves up. But there's a massive difference between self-love and arrogance.

When I got the students to read their new statements, written from the point of view of an inner cheerleader, the energy in the room became charged with excitement. Some of their teachers reported back to me that they were still buzzing in class hours afterwards.

This is the power of self-belief. It lights us up from the inside. And it makes me think that often, the deciding factor between success and failure comes down to the things our inner voice is telling us. I know that personally, when I finally managed to get my inner voice to be supportive enough to let me write a novel, it resulted in my first book deal. And once I'd got a book deal, I was able to prove my Inner Voice of Doom wrong: I *did* have what it takes to become a published writer.

So, the next time your inner voice starts with its fearful commentary, acknowledge that it's just scared and choose to make it come up with something a lot more encouraging - the kind of thing you would say to your own best friend.

A Beginner's Guide to Meditation

I've been meditating since I was about eighteen.

Not constantly, you understand - that would be one hell of a spiritual practice - but over the years, meditation has played an essential role in my happiness and well-being.

I've often heard friends joke that they only pray when times are tough - beginning their prayers with a sheepish, *'Sorry, God, I know it's been a while, but I promise I'll pray a whole lot more if you just do this one thing for me...'*

For many years, my meditation practice followed a similar pattern - when things were going well, I hardly bothered. What was the point? Things were going well, I was happy and besides, it frickin' hurts sitting cross-legged for hours on end. But when things started going badly, I'd be dusting that meditation pillow off faster than you could say 'om shanti'.

In the past few years I've started something really radical - I've started meditating every day, sometimes even twice a day! The results have been incredible, and that's why I've written this **Beginner's Guide to Meditation**. I want to share what I believe to be an incredible gift with you.

Here are some things I've learnt on the path to my regular meditation practice:

- *Many things in life are out of your control*

- *Even the things you think are within your control aren't*

- *This can make you feel really scared*

- *When you feel really scared you can start doing all kinds of things to try and cling on to a false sense of control*

- *When these don't work, you end up feeling even more scared*

- *So you become even more desperate in your attempts to regain control*

But the most important thing I've learnt is this: It's okay to be powerless.

In fact, once you get the hang of it, it's even kind of fun.

Think about it - if we embrace our powerlessness and if we accept that the only thing we can really control are our own thoughts and actions it is completely and utterly liberating.

Just imagine not being so affected by what others say or do. Just imagine being able to let go of life's disappointments and fears and rest in the knowledge that life has a knack of unfolding just fine once you release it from your mental stronghold.

Over the years I've tried many different meditations but the one I'm going to share with you here is my absolute fail-safe. It's so powerful in its simplicity.

Letting Go Meditation

Make sure you're somewhere nice and quiet where you're not going to be distracted.

Sit in as upright a position as possible (if your knees scream at the very thought of a cross-legged pose that's fine, just sit upright in a chair, spine straight, feet flat on the floor).

Place your hands on your knees, palms facing upwards.

Close your eyes.

Focus on your breathing - in through the nose and out through the mouth.

Once your breathing is calm and happening naturally with no effort, say the following words in your mind:

'*Let*' (on the in breath)

'*Go*' (on the out breath)

Let ... go

Let ... go

And as you repeat this mantra in your head, start to visualise any person or situation that you've been feeling powerless over.

Picture yourself letting go of them in whichever way suits you. (I like to see them as balloons being released into the sky, or leaves drifting away from me, down a river).

Let ... go

Feel your body start to relax as your mind lets go.

Enjoy the sensation of freedom this brings.

Let ... go

Let go of any associated feelings of anger and fear.

Feel nothing but love for the person or situation (this may seem massively difficult at first but keep trying - when it does happen it feels phenomenally liberating).

Let ... go

Try this for at least five minutes. When you're starting out, it may help to play some soothing instrumental music in the background to help you let go (*Top Tip: Metallica is NOT the best music to meditate to*).

The important thing to realise about meditation is that it isn't a quick fix; something to be done only when times are tough. To really see the benefit you have to make it a regular practice. And even then, I don't think you ever get to a point where life becomes a total breeze.

This is *life* we're talking about - crap happens. Meditation doesn't stop bad things from happening, but it does have a massive impact on how well you deal with them.

I'll finish with an example from my own life.

My son is eighteen and shortly off to uni. He's becoming an adult and my role as his mum is becoming a massive exercise in letting go. At times it's bloody difficult. At times, every fibre in my body is screaming not to. But I know that he needs to exert his independence and I need to take a step back. Stepping back to take a seat on my meditation pillow is helping massively right now. Instead of torturing myself over all the terrible things that might happen to him while he's out in the world living his life, meditation gives me a sense of peace and calm - and a deep sense that all will be well.

I hope it brings the same for you.

Just remember to:

Let ... go

In 2014 I started an advice column on my blog called Dear Dare to Dream. It ended up creating some of my most heart-felt - and popular - posts...

Dear Dare to Dream: Do I Need to go to Uni to be a Writer?

Dear Dare to Dream,

I am applying for university this year and I have chosen English degrees, including English language and linguistics and English language and creative writing. In relation to my dream career I would love to be a journalist and an author! (Which you are!) Would I need a degree in the field of English language to successfully achieve this? I was wondering if you perhaps have a degree in English and if that was worth it or if it had helped you (because it's going to put me in so much debt and I want to make sure it's worth it!).

Also, because I've been told they are not very stable/realistic jobs for me and it is hard to succeed in those fields, therefore I am considering becoming an English teacher with my degree. I know it's hard to succeed as an author and you have to be well skilled to be published so do you think this would be a better career option for me? It would be great to hear some advice from you on this subject - I'm sure you'll have experience or thoughts on it and I would love for you to share them with me.

Also, I've started writing on *Wattpad* but it's very hard to get recognition in a community full of millions of great writers, so do you have any advice you can give me on how I could attract readers. Thank you very much, I look forward to hearing from you! Have a great day!

M x

Dear M,

There was so much in your email I could relate to.

When I was your age I dreamt of being a writer and like you, applying to uni to study English seemed like the natural thing to do. I also harboured back-up plans of becoming a teacher, until someone threatened to break both my legs if I did(!), more on which later…

At first, I loved uni life but midway through my second year, things changed. I came from a much poorer background than most of my fellow students and while their parents were able to financially support them through their studies (some even providing credit cards and cars!) I was getting deeper and deeper into debt. Another thing that started getting to me was that the other students on my course who wanted to become writers all seemed to have contacts in that world already through their families. During holidays these contacts would give them work experience placements on newspapers or in publishing houses. I started to feel as if I didn't belong in that world and my Inner Voice of Doom started having a field day, telling me that I didn't have what it took to become a writer and I ought to give up immediately.

At the end of my second year I got a job in a shop and I never went back.

So when you talk about your concerns over the debt going to uni creates, I can answer you as someone who felt that debt so acutely I gave up on uni and very nearly gave up on my writing dream.

But things are different now.

Although today's student loans leave you thousands in debt they're not like the bank debt I ran up as a student, in that they're interest-free and you only have to start paying them back once you're earning a certain level of income. And the repayments are taken directly from your salary too so, in that sense, you could view your loan as a tax - far less scary than the prospect of spiralling interest rates and debt collectors.

You ask if you would need a degree in English to achieve your writing dreams and I'm living proof that no, you don't.

I may have given up on my writing dream when I dropped out of uni but my writing dream didn't give up on me.

As a fellow writer, I'm sure you can relate to this. When you've been bitten by the writing bug it's impossible to shake.

So I kept writing bits and pieces here and there and then I had a brainwave – I would treat writing just like any other occupation. Instead of viewing it as some kind of hallowed calling solely for people from wealthy backgrounds, I would view it exactly as I would view a career in plumbing or hair-dressing or customer services or computer programming. I would start at the bottom and work my way up to the top, with experience as my qualification.

I started writing short stories and articles and sending them off to magazines.

I started getting rejections.

And my Inner Voice of Doom started having a field day.

But thankfully I managed to ignore it and then I had my first story published, swiftly followed by my first article.

And after a few articles, I got my first non-fiction book deal.

My plan was working.

But it still felt like a massive leap to reach my ultimate dream – of becoming a novelist.

Then, like you, I considered going back to uni so that I could become a teacher.

How do you feel when you think about becoming a teacher, M?

When I thought of becoming a teacher I felt like a deflated balloon. But it seemed like the sensible and safe option. And by then I was a mum and the pressure to be sensible and safe was immense.

But then I had a lunch with my dad - a lunch that would go on to change everything.

I told him what I was thinking of doing.

His exact words to me were: *'If you give up your dream and become a teacher, I'll break both your legs.'*

Please note; my dad is a gruff Irishman with a very dark sense of humour. He didn't actually mean it - at least I don't *think* he did - but he knew how much writing meant to me and he didn't want me giving up on my dream.

And I don't want you giving up on yours either.

Because when you give up on your dreams you feel like a deflated balloon - and that's not good at all.

If, when you think about becoming a teacher, the prospect of educating and inspiring young people makes you feel fired up and alive, then I'd say it sounds like an excellent back-up plan.

But if you're only considering it out of fear and wanting to do the 'stable and realistic' thing then I'd urge you to put all of your energy into chasing your dream of becoming a writer.

You can go the uni route - getting a degree in English certainly won't hurt your writerly dreams - far from it.

Or you can do what I did and get a job that pays the bills and write every spare second you can, starting small and aiming big.

Take the student loan out of the equation for a moment. Imagine you won the lottery and had enough money to *buy* a university - how does the prospect of going to uni make you feel now?

When you think about learning about writing from the masters...

When you think about the new friends you'll make from all over the country...

When you think about the life experience and the adventure...

How does it make you feel?

If it makes you feel excited and alive; if the student loan is the only thing holding you back, then I'd say go for it.

The trick is to start using your feelings as a compass when it comes to your decision-making.

If something makes you feel excited and alive you know you're on the right path.

If it makes you feel dead inside, you know you're being steered by fear.

You say you've been told by others that being a writer or journalist are not stable or realistic jobs but this is *your* life you're living.

When you make your major decisions based on someone else's opinions you become a bit-player in their life story instead of the lead role in your own.

The truth is, it's hard to make a living purely from books but one of the joys of being a writer is that it opens up so many other exciting sources of income.

As well as writing, I coach other writers, I run writing workshops, I work as an editorial consultant, I give talks about writing. And I love doing all of these things.

Yes I have times when I worry about money, but I love the freedom of being my own boss and when I wake up in the morning I can't wait to get to work. How many people are lucky enough to be able to say that?

So in summary, M, you're at a time in your life where every decision feels vital and life changing and the sense of responsibility can be crippling.

But this truly isn't as heavy as it seems.

Not when you have a clear dream to aim for.

And your feelings as your guide.

If something goes wrong, if you start feeling unsettled, unhappy or deflated inside you can readjust your course.

Just never take your sights off your dream.

Write with passion and hope and authenticity and self-belief.

Write on *Wattpad*. Write a blog. Write on social media.

And slowly but surely, your readers will find you.

Trust that this will happen naturally. Don't try to force it.

Forced writing makes for forced reading.

If you keep the feelings EXCITED and ALIVE as your compass and WRITING as your destination you won't go wrong, whatever you decide to do.

Wishing you heaps of luck and happiness and success...

Siobhan x

Your True Face Will Always Be Smiling

Recently, someone asked me for some guidance regarding their life. They knew they were really unhappy with the way things were but they had no idea how they actually wanted their life to be. *'I feel as if I've completely lost sight of who I am,'* they told me.

This can be an all too common symptom of modern life. We become so busy just trying to make ends meet / keep relationships together / get through another day, that we completely lose sight of who we really are and what we really want.

There's an ancient Zen koan that provides the perfect solution to this modern dilemma *(a koan is a question / statement designed to encourage reflection and lead people to a higher level of understanding of themselves and their lives)* and it goes like this:

"Show me your original face - the face you wore before you were born."

In other words, take the time, in reflection or meditation, to get back to the real essence of you; your 'original face' unscarred by your life experiences and unmasked by your fears.

Let me give you an example of how this works.

Supposing you suffered the traumatic loss of a loved one at an early age. In your desire to protect yourself from similar future hurt you might decide to never fully love again. You might choose to put on a mask of indifference when it comes to matters of the heart.

Or it could be that as a child you dreamt of being an artist but then a barbed putdown from a teacher or friend left you convinced that you were no good at painting. As a result, you bury your dream so deep you forget you even had it.

There are countless ways in which life and the people we encounter along the way can pull us away from our authentic selves.

So how do we get back to our 'original face'? How do we remove the masks?

Some time spent in reflection can be very effective. If meditation doesn't float your boat then try writing about some of your earliest memories of yourself and what you loved to do. Think of yourself as an archaeologist, excavating the free-spirited child within. Have a brainstorm, literally scribbling down all the details you can think of. When I did this exercise I remembered that as a child I loved being outdoors. I loved going off on adventures on my bike, spending time in the woods, imagining up stories, dancing in my bedroom, making up tunes on my flute, and playing at being a minicab driver! It doesn't matter how silly or trivial the details might seem, you need to get them all down in order to recreate a clear picture of your 'original face'.
Try finding a photo of yourself as a child - one that captures your free and hopeful spirit. This can help both as a memory prompt and a goal, for it is this spirit you are trying to rekindle.

And once you've remembered who you really are, you can set about making the necessary changes to bring your life into alignment.

Strangely enough, I still haven't got round to becoming a minicab driver but when I remembered how much I used to love to dance, I enrolled in a local class and I'm now half way through training to become a dance teacher.

Whenever I'm dancing I feel completely joyful and alive and this I believe, is the true litmus test for living authentically.

Your original face will always be smiling...

*(From tiny blog posts entire books grow ... I ended up writing a book inspired by the Original Face koan. **True Face** was published by Faber & Faber in April 2015 and is full of tips and advice on how to get back to your authentic self.)*

Dance Yourself Happy

"Just as the ancients danced to call upon the spirits in nature, we too can dance to find the spirits within ourselves that have been long buried and forgotten."
Anna Halprin

In all the years I've been life-coaching I've discovered many great, sure-fire ways to help people feel happier.

One of the best of these is gratitude.

And another is dance.

Now, anyone who has ever pointed their disco finger in the air to *Saturday Night Fever* knows that dancing is a great way to get those feel-good endorphins pumping.

But what I've realised over the past year and a half as I've been training to become a dance teacher is that if you combine the physical act of dance with a positive thinking exercise you're guaranteed a legal high even better than chocolate (and as someone whose motto is: *Cut me and I bleed cocoa*, I don't say that lightly).

And as I've found gratitude to be a sure-fire short-cut to joy, a dance of gratitude can boost your happiness levels in mere minutes.

Here are a few quick guidelines before you start, to make sure you get the most from the exercise:

- This will only work if you're able to totally lose yourself in the moment, so make sure you won't be interrupted. (Trust me, there's nothing worse than free-styling round your living room, losing yourself in the moment, only to be interrupted by a family member shouting: *'Mum, where's my football kit / lunch / hamster?'*)

- This type of dancing has got nothing to do with slick moves and precision choreography - it's all about doing whatever the hell you feel like doing and going wherever the music takes you. So let all inhibitions go.

- I've recommended several pieces of music that are perfect for this exercise below, but if you would rather choose your own then make sure it's something uplifting and that you won't be distracted by the lyrics. *Girlfriend in a Coma* by The Smiths is probably not advisable (unless of course, you are grateful that your girlfriend is in a coma - but then you would probably need more help than this book could provide...)

- Make sure you are barefoot

- Make sure your eyes are closed throughout (to avoid distractions)

When you're ready to begin place your right hand over your heart (your heart is on the left side of your chest for those of you who skipped biology).

And place your left hand on your stomach.

Take a few slow, deep breaths in through the nose and out through the mouth and relax.

Feel really present in your body.

Then press play and when the music starts, let your feet slowly find the rhythm and raise your hands in the air.

Keeping your eyes closed, let the music guide you.

And as you dance, start thinking about all of the things and all of the people you are grateful for.

Think about them slowly and one at a time and focus on how grateful you are that they are in your life.

Express these feelings through your dance.

Then, if you want to take this exercise even deeper, start thinking about the people and/or situations currently causing you stress.

As you continue to dance see if you can find ways to feel grateful for them too.

What lessons have they taught you?

How have they helped you grow stronger, kinder, wiser?

Feel free to do this exercise for as long as you like, dancing deeper and deeper into gratitude and joy.

Recommended Music for Dancing With Gratitude

Wonderful World, Louis Armstrong
Feeling Good, Nina Simone
Singin' in the Rain, Gene Kelly
Do You realise,The Flaming Lips
Happy, Pharrell Williams
I Hope You Dance, Lee Ann Womack
Flashdance What a Feeling, Irene Cara
Flying Without Wings, Westlife

Dancing With Fear

When I started writing the *Dare to Dream* blog it was very important to me that it didn't become one of those *ra-ra* life coach-y sermons that waxed lyrical about how darned perfect my life was. And how darned perfect yours could be too if you only attended one of my workshops / talks / read one of my books.

It was very important to me that the things I write here should be authentic and from the heart during good times *and* bad.

Yes, the blog is called *Dare to Dream* but the truth is, sometimes our dreams don't come true, no matter how hard we dare. And sometimes, when we get so close to true happiness we can practically hear the soaring violins, our fears come rushing back with a vengeance and threaten to derail everything.

This is what happened to me recently.

My life had been going so sweetly and then, like gatecrashers intent on wrecking the party (and stubbing their cigarettes out on all your best furniture) my fears came flooding in.

I'm sure I'm not alone in experiencing this.

How often have you been poised at the edge of something great and then fear has hit you like a sledgehammer?

And before you know it, your good ol' Inner Voice of Doom has taken over, bellowing: *'You can't do that / be that / have that!'*

So, what should we do when fear gets us in a choke-hold?

In the past I've tried to fight it but that usually only makes it worse.

The fears become magnified. Not to get all life coach-y on you, but *what you resist, definitely does persist.*

So this time round I'm trying a different approach.

I've decided to go with the fear.

To let it in...

...and then let it out.

And the way I'm letting it out is to write about it (in the poem below).

I've also done something really mature, and so unlike me in these situations - instead of bottling it up and leaving it to fester I talked about it with someone close to me.

And now I'm writing about it and talking about it with all of you.

And in doing these things, I'm finding that my fears are starting to shrink.

To go back to the cigarette-stubbing gatecrasher analogy, if you open the door to them, if you say, '*hey, do your worst, I never liked that crappy furniture anyway,*' right away you are taking back your power.

So if fear is threatening to ruin your party, why don't you try the same?

Write and talk the hell out of it, until there's nothing left to see and, to quote from my poem below, you're hopefully pulled back into the dance.

DANCING WITH FEAR

I thought I'd escaped you this time,
Thought I'd slipped from your shadows unseen
As I danced on into the light.
But now a cloud passes over the sun,
And I freeze, mid-pirouette.

Your whisper circles me like a chill breeze,
Cutting straight to my heart.
'Who are you to deserve such joy?'
'Who are you to dance with such grace?'

I close my eyes and teeter.
In the furthest corners of my mind
Poisonous memories raise themselves from the dead.
I feel myself shrinking,
Falling.
The darkness smothering.

I reach around blindly for a hand to help me.
To pull me back into the dance.

So What if I'm Weird? It's Frickin' Wonderful!

'Do you ever think we're weird?' I asked my son as we walked along the towpath.

We'd just spent about fifteen minutes creating our own version of Cockney rhyming slang using the names of Communist leaders (Commie rhyming slang).

'Yep,' he replied with a laugh.

'Don't ever change,' I told him.

Because here's the thing:

Being weird is wonderful.

There are lots of ways in which I'm weird. Here are just a selection...

I get high on words - I really do. If just the right words are placed in just the right order it makes every cell in my body grin.

I spend hours some days in the company of imaginary friends - imaginary friends who often *but not always*, end up in my books.

Once, I danced for half an hour in the street - I'd had some great news that made me feel like dancing. The friend I was with pulled his car over, put some salsa music on the stereo and we got out and threw our own private street party. It might have looked weird but it felt wonderful.

Three years ago, I accidentally gave up drinking. I say 'accidentally' because I did the dry January thing and I never started again. I know that a lot of people think I'm weird for choosing a mineral water over a merlot but it feels wonderful being clear-headed and full of energy all the time.

Sometimes when I go running around the fields where I live I fling my arms out like a pair of wings and pretend to be a plane. It might look crazy but it's beyond exhilarating.

I enjoy being single. This, I'm sure, makes me really weird in the Noah's Ark-style, two-by-two world we live in but right now, I'm loving having the time and space to devote to my son and my writing and other adventures.

Sometimes I lie down on lock gates and gaze at the sky. Some people might think this behaviour freakishly weird but I'm telling you, listening to the water and watching the clouds skim by feels awesome.

I have been known to write letters to my future partner. I might enjoy being single but I'm a true romantic at heart; I believe in soul mates and twin flames and paths being destined to cross. Writing a letter to someone you don't even know yet might seem crazy but I love wondering what he's doing, where he is and how we're going to meet. I love believing in magic, however weird it might seem.

It's occurred to me, writing this post, that my happiest, most memorable times are when I'm being 'weird'.

But right now, it seems as if all the world wants is for us to fit in neatly, dumbed down by reality TV, churning out selfie after selfie, performing our lives as some kind of carefully choreographed show-reel on social media.

The army of airbrushers invade our minds, planting insecurities with every concave stomach and flawless face.

'How to Get a Bikini Body' is deemed more important than *'How to Live a Life of Adventure'*.

Weird = bad and bland = good.

And statistics show - again and again and again - that we've never felt so depressed or anxious or full of self-loathing.

But what if 'weird' wasn't weird at all?

What if it's how we're truly meant to be?

What if weird = our uniqueness? Our originality?

What if we lived in a world where being different was celebrated and encouraged?

A world where people regularly danced in the street.

Or ran like aeroplanes.

Or talked and acted and lived and loved exactly how they wanted to.

Wouldn't that be wonderful?

As Johnny Depp once said: "*I think everybody's weird. We should all celebrate our individuality and not be embarrassed or ashamed of it.*"

So today, celebrate your weirdness.

Refuse to be squashed into a life that just isn't big or exciting or interesting enough.
Until next time...

Ciao-cescu! (*Commie rhyming slang for good-bye*)

Little Changes, One by One, Make One Big Change

Today I'm so happy to welcome my first ever guest to the Dare to Dream blog.

Michelle Richards is a friend, work colleague and total inspiration to me, and I'm delighted to be able to share her story with you here.

In 2009, Michelle was diagnosed with leukaemia and plunged into a three year fight for survival. Throughout that time she confronted her diagnosis with her own unique brand of feistiness and humour and refused to give up on her dreams for the future – even when the doctors told her she was about to die...

Welcome to Dare to Dream, Michelle. Can you tell us a bit about your life prior to getting ill?

Well, I was just an ordinary girl really, I loved being active and playing sport. I had just got married and had spent five weeks travelling around Thailand for my honeymoon. I was working full time as a Marketing Director and loved to go out of the weekends. I was turning thirty and was just starting to think about having a family in the near future.

What were the first signs of your illness?

I had a sharp stabbing pain under the left side of my rib. At first the doctors thought I had a bout of shingles. The pain didn't go away and then my belly began to look bloated like I was pregnant. After a blood test, a subsequent high white blood count and spleen the size of an unborn baby, I was diagnosed. With hindsight, I can now see that before these more immediate symptoms popped up, I had also lost lots of weight and was feeling tired all the time.

How did you initially react to your diagnosis? Was there a moment when you can remember deciding that it wasn't going to beat you?

At first I was in shock, I was taken into hospital for two weeks to stabilise my condition. I had a childhood friend who had suffered with leukaemia so my first thought was, *this is crazy, I already know someone who has had leukaemia, I can't have it too!* And then, as the hours passed and the reality started to dawn on me, all I kept chanting to everyone was, 'If Helen can beat it, so can I!'

I was then told that in 95% of cases, medication would be able to hold my condition at bay long term and I could carry on living a normal life. So after the initial shock, I tried to do everything in my power to make sure this 'thing' inside me that I had to take medication for, never stopped me achieving anything. I worked harder, I trained harder. I raised money for Leukaemia and Lymphoma research by running a triathlon, I was head-hunted for a new job position. I was sticking two fingers up at this insideous disease.

Then bam! After two years, it turned out I was in the unlucky 5% - my condition progressed into an aggressive, life-threatening form of Leukaemia, which left me with only one week to live and without two rounds of chemotherapy, full body radiation and a bone marrow transplant I was a goner. Then I had to deal with the 'death shock' all over again. But this time I'd had practice. I was determined to beat it. I was going to stare death straight in the eyes and not blink or ever look away. Whatever cancer was going to throw at me, I was ready to suck it up and spit it back out.

For the next year and a half I definitely made the best of a bad situation. My family, support nurses and I laughed, joked and occasionally cried. We were creative in finding things to do and appreciated every moment we spent together.

What helped you to stay so positive throughout your illness?

Every bad experience was turned into a joke and laughed at, and our family mantra was '*Man up, Mich!*' It made me feel indestructible - even though my blood was as much use to me as a chocolate tea pot; my blood was killing me!

I also had a mentor who helped me through the bad times. Her name was Elizabeth and she had been through the same experience six years prior to me. She was my rock and I was able to talk to her about my treatment and get advice. It helped so much to know someone who really knew what I was going through. I respected her opinion more than anyone else's. I also took inspiration from other people I knew who had been through life threatening issues and had come out the other side to tell the tale. I'd think to myself, *if they can do it, why can't I?*

There must have been some incredibly tough times though. Did you ever reach a rock bottom point during your illness?

Yes, most definitely. The day the doctors told me my first round of chemo hadn't worked and that I should go home and spend the rest of my time with my family before I passed away.

I love the story of how you overcame this particular obstacle. Please can you share it with us here?

I told the doctor in no uncertain terms that I'd had worse hangovers than his chemotherapy - I didn't even get the runs! - and that he should go back and double the dose. The doctor told me that the chances of a second round of chemo working were very slim, but I was willing to take the chance. I wasn't going to give up! In the end I tried a different type of chemo, which thankfully did work and allowed me to move forward to my stem cell transplant.

What role did your dreams for the future play in your recovery?

Dreams of my future played a huge part in my recovery, due to the simple fact that I could SEE my future in my mind. I could SEE me doing things with my family, I could SEE me healthy and most of all, I could SEE me laughing! How can anyone give up on the dreams of their future?

So, now that you're thankfully in recovery, please can you tell us a bit more about your dreams?

My short-term dreams include travelling more. I managed to get to Indonesia for three weeks over Christmas and I would like to eventually be in a position to share my time between Australia and the UK. This is going to take lots of hard work and I am going to learn a new occupation which will allow me to work from anywhere in the world.
I'm also currently training for a non-stop 24 hour, 100km hike to raise money and awareness for Leuka, the research facility at the hospital that saved my life. (I dream about completing that one without getting any blisters!)

I would love to meet my stem cell donor sometime this year (if he agrees to disclose his details).

And I am back working, playing sport and putting the pieces of my life back together with my family.

Do you have any advice for readers of this blog, based on what you have been through?

You have to remember that you can't fulfill all of your dreams at once. You need to look at the little things that you can do to change the direction of your life. These little changes, one by one, make one big change and when you look back, you're in a much better place than when you started.

The way I see it, the world is out there for the taking and I am going to grab it with both hands.

Tragically, Michelle passed away in 2014, but in the years she was in recovery she achieved a phenomenal amount. She travelled, she trained as a financial investor, she got a new job, she completed her sponsored walk from London to Brighton and raised thousands for charity. And she never once lost her wicked sense of humour. She grabbed the world with both hands and she is a shining example to us all. I hope you've been inspired by her words...

Museum Musing: In the Face of Death, Cherish Life

Recently, I was lucky enough to take part in a project for radio station Resonance FM at the British Museum. I was one of six writers invited to come to a private viewing of the Pompeii exhibition and then write about what we'd seen. There were some beautiful sculptures and pieces of artwork on display, but for me the most moving and powerful element of the exhibition was the human story. Reading about and seeing how suddenly and horrifically the citizens of Pompeii and Herculaneum met their deaths following the eruption of Mount Vesuvius has left a lasting impression on me. During the excavation of Pompeii, plaster was used to fill the voids between the ash layers that had once held human bodies. At the end of the exhibition you came to a room housing some of these casts; people frozen forever in their moment of death. Although most of the casts were made from plaster, there was one of a woman that had been made from resin and she glowed a beautiful shade of pale amber. Next to her lay the bracelet, ring and Venus hairpin she'd been wearing that fateful day. Up until that point I'd been wondering what to write about. Now I knew. I sat down in the darkness beside her and the words flowed...

Who were you Resin Lady?
What were your dreams?
Your lies?
Your truths?
When the firey rocks rained down that day
I hope love swooped in,
Like Venus on your hairpin
Shimmering light in the dusty darkness
To come and take you home.
Your body may be gone,
But your energy has left an imprint
Not even Vesuvius could destroy.

A glowing amber beacon,
A permanent reminder
To cherish life
And make every moment count.

Although what happened in Pompeii was horrific and extraordinary, the fact is, life can be snatched from us at any moment. But, rather than come away from the exhibition feeling depressed, I felt strangely inspired. For me personally, the Pompeii exhibition held a vital lesson.

It literally beamed a spotlight on death and in doing so, highlighted the importance of life.

It also raised a question I think we should ask ourselves every day: **What kind of imprint do I want to leave behind?**

Banish Fear in Your Career and Follow Your Bliss

Lately, I've been thinking a lot about Love and Fear - and how we tend to be engaged in a permanent battle between the two.

The obvious arena in which we do this is our relationships, but it struck me recently that our work lives can often be blighted by fear too.

And just as we need to keep guiding our relationships back to love, the same is true of our work life - if we're to have a rich and fulfilling career.

When I started out as a writer I often felt trapped in the following maze of fear:

- *Will publishers like my book enough to offer me a book deal?*

- *Will stores like my book enough to stock it?*

- *Will readers like my book enough to buy and recommend it?*

- *Will I sell enough copies to keep providing for myself and my son?*

Then, after four books with a major UK publisher, my worst fears were realised. My fourth book didn't sell as well as my publisher had hoped and I was dropped.

When this happened I was devastated. And plagued by fear. *What was I going to do? How was I going to provide for my son?*

But fears are a bit like the imaginary monsters from our childhood that we were convinced lived under the bed.

Sometimes it's only when you're face to face with your worst fear that you realise it had all been a figment of your imagination.

Obviously I hadn't imagined the fact that I'd been dropped by my publisher. That part was all too real. But I had imagined an ensuing life of poverty and doom and gloom.

And the reality turned out to be anything but.

For the next couple of years I made helping others the sole focus of my career. I trained as a life coach and started running numerous writing workshops and events, helping other writers follow their dream. And in doing so, my career became rooted in a place of love rather than fear. I made so many new and fantastic friends during that time and my house became a buzzing focal point for creative get-togethers, workshops and parties. It's left me with a montage of happy memories I'll never forget.

And when I did pluck up the courage to write another novel, it too came out of a desire to help others and a place of love.

In my role as a writer in residence at a high school I'd been working a lot with teens. It was a real reminder of how dramatic and tough this time of life can be and I had the sudden urge to write fiction for young people as way of helping them through this mine-field.

My motivation this time round was purely for the love of writing and a desire to help. So much so that when my first young adult novel *Dear Dylan* was finished, I turned down a two book deal and self-published it so that I could give away the e-book for free.

I truly believe that - whatever our career - when we're motivated by love (for others or for the work itself) and are unhindered by fear, we do our very best work.

Despite being self-published, *Dear Dylan* went on to win a national award.

This in turn led to me being offered another traditional book deal.

And so now, even with my thirteenth book about to be published and my fourteenth due out next year, I'm still all too aware that it could end tomorrow.

But this time round, I won't become lost in that maze of fear.

This time round, I know that the things that seem the most scary usually present us with incredible opportunities for growth and exciting new beginnings.

Although it might sound cheesy, when you put love for others or the work itself at the heart of what you do, there's no room left for fear.

If you feel that you're currently letting fear rule your career, try using the following questions to help you steer it back to love:

- What hobby / activity really makes you come alive?

- Is there any way that you could make a living from this?

- How could you use your skills and life experience to help others?

- What would your dream job be?

- What small step could you take today towards making that dream job a reality?

- Is there any way that you could overlap your current job with your dream job until the latter hopefully takes off?

- How could you bring more love into your current job?

Walking To Be Still

"If you seek creative ideas go walking. Angels whisper to a man when he goes for a walk."
Raymond I. Myers

If you ever want to see what the living dead look like, go for a ride on the London Underground during rush hour.

Seriously.

Two days a week I work in London as an editorial consultant and two days a week I am plunged into commuter hell.

There's something so depressing about being part of that sea of suited misery, flowing through the network of grimy tunnels to be deposited into characterless office blocks day after day after day.

There's no doubt in my mind that commuting is very bad for the soul.

Very bad indeed.

This morning a man actually flung his briefcase in front of me in a bid to stop me getting to the one vacant seat on the train before him.

Yesterday, a woman practically mounted me from behind in her rush to get through the ticket barrier.

But it's not just commuting that's getting people so uptight.

Life is stressful.

Life is chaotic.

Life makes people grumpy and anxious and rude.

It really ought to come with a health warning.

But there's something we all can do to unwind, anytime, anywhere, and for free.

I'm talking about walking.

When I had a dog, I had to go walking at least twice a day come rain or shine and I loved it.

There's something about the repetitive process of putting one foot in front of the other that's incredibly soothing.

Walking brings a slow, melodic rhythm to the most discordant of days.

It's like soothing jazz piano after hours of thrash metal.

Of course, we're often so uptight from the rest of our lives that we bring that same highly charged energy to our walking - witness the nuclear-style rage induced on any London street when a tourist dares to meander or even worse, stop dead to consult their map.

For some people, walking is just an excuse to get even more tightly coiled.

I pity those fools.

Because when you know how, walking is one of the best ways to achieve stillness and inner peace in existence.

Tonight, on my way back from London, I decided to walk home from the station along the canal.

Because I wanted to get the most from my walk, I stopped off to buy an ice-cream on the way.

Every so often a runner would pound by, a look of grim determination upon their face. I just took another mouthful of ice-cream and watched the ducks.

With every meandering step, I felt the tension of the day seeping from my muscles.

With every breath-taking glimpse of nature's beauty, I felt my soul begin to sing.

By the time I reached home, thirty minutes later, I felt completely renewed.

So, how do you walk to be still?

Let me present you with this handy guide:

- Walking to be still is not power-walking

- It is more a meander

- Establish a gentle rhythm to your steps

- Synchronise your breathing

- If you find yourself stressing or engaging in endless mind chatter try repeating a mantra in your head

- A mantra with two syllables is good because you can keep step in time

- Try saying *'let go'* or *'love life'* (or *'ice cream'*)

- Keep your head up and your eyes wide open

- Look all around you

- Be right there - in the moment

- If there is something troubling you, imagine that you are literally walking away from it *(this one can be very effective)*

- With every step you take, picture your problem fading into the distance behind you

- Smile

- Smile even more

- If there's a goal you really want to achieve, imagine that you're walking towards it

- Imagine that you're walking, step by gentle step, into a happier future

- And know that you are

Plant Seeds of Joy and See How They Grow

"When you do things from your soul, you feel a river moving in you, a joy."
Rumi

One of the biggest problems with Western society is that joy is all too often associated with things that are not immediately attainable: *the dream job, the ideal home, the soul mate, winning the lottery.*

And so, if we find ourselves in a *dead end job, a crappy bedsit, single, broke*, we can feel like big fat failures who surely aren't entitled to any happiness at all.

But the truth is, we all have the capacity to feel joy at any given moment, regardless of our personal circumstances.

Obviously, if you're currently being stampeded by a herd of elephants while some eejit plays Cliff Richard on a loop (especially if it's that *'Christmas time, mistletoe and wine'* one), then maybe this doesn't apply.

But for most other situations, here are some simple, sure-fire ways to create joy right now.

View Life like a Child

Have you ever seen a group of little kids sitting round in playgroup frowning and saying things like, *'You know, I'm just not in the mood for the sandpit today, I've got way too much on my mind.'* Or, *'Oh my God, which fool got the paint out? Now I'm going to ruin my new dungarees!'*

Kids have an endless capacity for creating joy - and getting messy. When they look at the world they don't see endless problems, they see limitless fun.

Puddles are for splashing in, trees are for climbing, a plain old cardboard box instantly becomes a racing car / play-house / fort.

So the first vital step in creating your own joy is to start thinking like a kid again.

What did you love to do as a kid?

Where did you love to play?

Take a moment to close your eyes and relive some favourite childhood memories.

How could you bring some of that same playful spirit into your adult life?

Jot down your ideas in a notebook.

What fun thing could you do in the next twenty-four hours to bring your inner child out to play?

Try to do at least one thing a day that satisfies the big kid in you.

Create Your Own Happy Dance

For this exercise to work you have to forget about all notions of looking cool. The only shapes you're going to be throwing here are some serious mis-shapes. The idea of a happy dance is that it should make you laugh your head off. So throw yourself into the music without giving a damn about how you look.

I've recommended some of my favourite happy dance tunes below but you may well have some of your own. Pick a song that makes your heart sing, with a seriously funky beat, push all the furniture back - and dance free.

Keep on dancing till you've lost all control. In our buttoned-up world you have no idea how liberating this can be.

If at any point during your dance you catch yourself thinking, *hey, that move I just did was pretty damn cool,* then it's time to start again. You mustn't be thinking about how you look at all. Just let go and let rip.

(Top tip: if you happen to be discovered mid happy dance, tell your interloper that you're trying to contact your ancient shamanic panther guide - this should soon get rid of them.)
My recommended happy dance tunes: *Bare Necessities* from The Jungle Book, *Happy* by Pharrell Williams, *Flashdance What a Feeling* by Irene Cara and the theme tune from *Ghostbusters* (please don't judge).

Paint a Happy Picture

When's the last time you painted anything - other than your nails or the walls?

Invest in a cheap set of paints and some paper.

Before you begin, take a few moments to get into a happy zone.

Close your eyes and think back to one of the most joyful times in your life.

Really relive it with all of your senses. What did you see, hear, taste, smell, feel?

Then, when you're ready, open your eyes and start to paint, letting your instincts be your guide.

As with your happy dance, don't over-think your picture.

Don't get hung up on what it *should* look like.

Just express sheer joy through the colours and the shapes.

Again, as with the dance, the messier you can get with this, the better.

If for whatever reason, you can't get hold of any paints, try taking a photo that encapsulates joy for you.

When I did this exercise I took a picture of a field of daisies. For me, daisies always symbolise joy. So much so that when I was a kid I begged my parents to rename me Daisy and wrote *'This book belongs to Daisy Curham'* inside every one of my books as a blatant act of rebellion when they refused. What could you take a photo of today that would be guaranteed to make you smile?

When you've taken your picture use it as the screensaver on your phone as a constant reminder to be happy.

Immerse Yourself in Happy Words

Ultimately, our unhappy thoughts are made up of unhappy words. So try rewriting them by immersing yourself in uplifting words.

Either your own:

- Write a list of all the people and things you are grateful for

- Write about the achievements you are most proud of

- Free-write about your perfect day, using all of the senses to really bring your description to life

Or you can lose yourself in the joyful words of others.

- Re-read a favourite children's book

- Read some uplifting poetry

- Copy out some uplifting quotes that make your heart sing

Here are some favourites of mine to get you started:

"I don't think of all the misery, but of the beauty that remains."
Anne Frank

"Don't cry because it's over, smile because it happened."
Dr Seuss

"Sometimes your joy is the source of your smile, but sometimes your smile can be the source of your joy." **Thich Nhat Hanh**

So today, dance, paint, read and write with the energy and imagination of a child.

Plant seeds of joy and see how they grow...

How to Create a Summer of Freedom and Adventure

"And so with the sunshine and the great bursts of leaves growing on the trees, just as things grow in fast movies, I had that familiar conviction that life was beginning over again with the summer."

F. Scott Fitzgerald

Here in the UK, we're enjoying our first proper summer in thirty-six years - or at least for us sun-starved Brits, that's what it feels like. We have now had weeks of virtually uninterrupted sunshine and I don't know about you, but, like the quote from *The Great Gatsby* above, it feels as if life is beginning all over again.

I feel renewed...

energised...

ALIVE!

Do you remember how, as kids on the last day of summer term, we'd race through the school gates and into an endless, sun-bleached adventure? Sand-castles and sun-cream, swing-ball and paddling. Fishing nets on sticks, ice-cream in cones, bright pink sticks of rock and electric-blue slush puppies that gave you sticky mouths and brain-freeze. Playing out till dark; hide and seek and tag, kiss-chase and camping. Making tents out of bed-sheets and pillows of mown grass, our skin and hair smelling of trapped sunshine.

For. Six. Whole. Weeks.

It seemed like forever.

And now, here we are on the cusp of August - thirty-one ripe days of summer before us.

So, how can you squeeze every last feel-good drop from the coming month?

How can you recapture the sense of adventure and renewal you felt as a school's out child?

First of all, you need to set yourself an intention.

Take a piece of paper and write on it:

"I declare this August to be my SUMMER OF . . . ."

Then fill in the gap with the word that resonates most with you:

FUN
LOVE
FREEDOM
ADVENTURE
HAPPINESS
GROWTH

Or choose one of your own.

Back at the start of last August, I declared my own summer to be one of adventure. I wanted to recapture the sense of freedom and excitement summer always instilled in me as a child.

Just by setting this intention and making sure I lived by it every day led to one of the richest, most fun months I'd had in ages.

Like my childhood summers, I spent the majority of it outside.

I went to festivals.

I went orienteering in the wilds of Sussex.

I relocated my office to a corner of the back garden.

I played hide and seek in the woods and meditated in a secret garden.

And in living like a free-spirited child again, I felt layers of myself peeling away.

All of the crap accumulated during the uptight winter months was shed like old skin.

And I found that my childlike spirit of adventure began spilling over into every area of my life.

I rehauled my work plans, pitched a very different book idea to a publisher (which went on to become *True Face*), had my long hair cut short, and set up a savings account to pay for an overseas adventure.

I no longer rushed about like a lunatic, I did things like stop and feed the ducks on my way home from work.

I lay and gazed at the sky for literally hours on end.

And yet creatively, I'd never been more productive.

It's as if the warmth of the sun was causing ideas to spread like wild flowers in my mind.

So, if you feel your summer has been passing you by...

If you still feel caught on life's treadmill...

Make it your intention today to seize this summer.

To carpe the hell out of every last diem.

Let the sun relax and rejuvenate you.

Get outside and adventure.

Take a week off social media.

Take a moment to smell the roses.

Take *many* moments to smell the roses.

Paddle in the sea.

Build a sand castle and decorate it with shells.

Go exploring in the woods.

Leave a trail of arrows made from sticks.

Have a picnic.

Make a daisy chain.

Spend fun times with family and friends.

And above all...

live, love and laugh like a sun-kissed child.

When I Grow Up...

Do you remember when you were little and adults would ask you what you wanted to be or do when you grew up?

And when you answered, you would blurt out your biggest wildest, most swashbucklingly bright dreams.

Because you were still ruled by your imagination.

And optimism.

And a thirst for fun and adventure.

Then you grew up and life happened and society taught you all about the importance of R.E.S.P.O.N.S.I.B.I.L.I.T.Y

And your biggest, wildest, most swashbuckingly bright dreams began to fade to grey.

Well not any more, *Dare to Dreamers*!

Today I want you to start dreaming like a child again.

I'm going to ask you what you want to do when you grow up and I want you to answer with all the imagination and crazy sass of a kid.

So please, no '*I want to take out an endowment mortgage*'.

I'll kick things off with a few of mine:

When I grow up I want to...

Build a house out of sticks and live in it with a pet squirrel named Sinbad

Be a superhero pirate with a cussing parrot on my shoulder

Take a trip in a hot air balloon and drop mysterious notes down to the people below

Eat cake for breakfast, lunch and dinner

Find a message in a bottle from a shipwrecked sailor - and go to his rescue

Ride a Harley Davidson across America singing 'Born to be Wild'

Live on a beach, with the sea lullabying me to sleep each night

Okay, now it's over to you.

What do you want to be or do when *you* grow up?

Dare to Ditch Dastardly Doubt

"Our doubts are traitors and make us lose the good we oft might win, by fearing to attempt."

William Shakespeare

If there's one thing I hate even more than pickled onions it's doubt.

Doubt is like the sneakiest of back-stabbers, loving to deliver a killer blow to your dreams when you least expect it.

Everyone suffers from moments of doubt - even the most confident of kick-butting go-getters - but the crucial difference comes in how we deal with it.

Do you brush doubt off?

Or do you let it consume you and sabotage your goals?

Several times in the past I've let doubt run the show and given up on certain dreams.

The first was when I was at university - my doubts that I could ever make it as a writer led to me dropping out after two years.

And currently, as I'm in the middle of developing a new online business, I find myself suddenly being plagued by doubt again.

Everything had been going so well.

I'd come up with a business idea that I feel so passionately about I've been doing crazy things, like setting my alarm for 5AM (AM standing for ACTUAL MORNING) just so I can do some work on it before a full day in the office.

This business idea has got me more excited than seeing Bruce Springsteen do *Jungle Land* live at Hard Rock Calling - and that got me so excited I hugged a psychotic looking stranger with a pit bull tattoo on his neck.

So imagine my horror when, just as I'm about to launch myself into creating my first product, doubt starts whispering slyly in my ear.

'What if it doesn't work?'
'What if everyone hates it?'
'What if you aren't able to market it properly?'
'What if you get NO customers?'
'What if you fail?!!!'

But this time, I'm determined not to let doubt run the show - or *ruin* the show.

And this is how I'm going to do it *(yep, it's handy, print-out-and-keep time)*.

How to Ditch Dastardly Doubt

- Instead of listening to doubt's 'what ifs', ask yourself what would happen if you let doubt win. When I dropped out of uni I ended up working for the complaints department of a frozen food company where people sent me the dead critters they'd found in their ice-cream. Nuff said.

- Write a list of all the reasons why you want to achieve the particular dream in question. My business idea would enable me to help loads of people. It would be massively rewarding and bring variety and adventure into my life on a large scale. It would also enable me to spend way more time in America - and achieve another life-long dream in the process.

- When you have your list of reasons why, stick it up somewhere you'll see it every day.

- Add pictures to it. If your dream is to start a cake shop, stick up pictures of cupcakes. If your dream is to become a travel writer, stick up pictures of far-flung beaches. Creating a visual representation of your dream can play a very powerful role in countering doubt.

- Stop making it about you. And by that I mean focus solely on who or what your dream would benefit. Strongly identifying a need for what you want to do is one of the most effective ways of getting doubt to shut the hell up. And even if your dream is all about you - for example it could be that you want to go back-packing for a year - then think of how your experiences might ultimately help others. The bottom line is, achieving a dream will make you feel incredibly happy and fulfilled, which will make you incredibly nice and inspiring to be around.

- Remind yourself that everyone experiences doubt and that the people who succeed in achieving their dreams are the ones who have learnt how to put doubt on mute.

And if you can't take my word for it, look at the quote at the top of this piece and take Shakespeare's.

Doubt is a traitor.

It sabotages your happiness; planting mental landmines amongst your dreams.

But the great news is, we always have the choice over how we react.

So keep on daring to dream and ditching the doubt. Every. Single. Day.

Why it's OK to Mess Up … And How to Make a Speedy Recovery

So, you're eight days into your *wheat-free, protein-free, FOOD-free, bikini-body diet* and then, as you walk past the bakers, you hear a red velvet cupcake sending you telepathic messages saying 'EAT ME! EAT ME NOW!' And before you know it, you're chin-deep in frosting.

Or, you finally find the courage to end a toxic relationship, only to find yourself two weeks and two hundred Adele ballads later sending a 'missing you' text.

Or, you've promised yourself that this weekend you are finally going to begin work on your novel / home improvement project / fitness campaign, only to find yourself slumped in front of a *Netflix* binge again.

And then, before you know it, your thoughts are sending you hurtling on the down escalator of doom.

I'm so rubbish!

I can't stick at anything!

I'm such a loser!

Better order myself a burkini!

Better cancel the holiday!

Now I've sent that text I'll never regain my self-respect!

I can't get anything done!

I might as well live vicariously via The Good Wife – she has way better hair! Etc…

I was having a conversation with my dad once and he said he could never understand why people who manage to give up smoking for months or even years, have one crafty cig on a night out and that's it - they're back smoking twenty a day. 'Why can't they just accept that they had a slip-up?' my dad asked. 'Why can't they focus on the fact that they've only had one smoke in two years rather than think, *I've had one smoke, I have no willpower*?'

Why, indeed.

I guess the quick answer is, we are way too swift to be way too hard on ourselves.

But why?

Maybe it's because we set such impossibly high standards for ourselves.

Women are brain-washed into thinking that to be seen in swimwear we have to obtain figures that are only achievable through near-starvation or chronic air-brushing.

Movies and magazines and the media bombard us with the notion that being single is sad, or a sign of failure. Thereby creating a culture where bad relationship choices are seen as preferable to the 'no relationship' choice.

And everywhere we turn, we are told of the importance of success. If we aren't constantly doing or achieving then we have to be failing – right?

Wrong.

Because this constant striving for perfection is completely impractical.

We are human beings.

Humans *being*.

And sometimes the being part gets messy.

Sometimes it just isn't possible to meet the exacting standards we set ourselves.

Sometimes we mess up.

But so what?

We all do it.

All of us.

So instead of beating ourselves up, we need to learn how to go with it, accept it and then bounce back.

If you eat a cake when you're on a diet, *enjoy every last crumb*.

Then go back to the diet.

One cake in a week of carrots is actually a massive achievement when you stop to think about it.

If you slip-up in your love life, take it as a reassuring sign that you have feelings and emotions. That you are *human*.

Then draw a line under it and move on.

If you don't get your to-do list done, enjoy the break from the grind, then write a new one for a new day.

And if you find yourself spiralling down into thoughts of doom and gloom, try these sure-fire ways to break the descent:

- *Get physical*: go for a run, walk, dance and literally shake your negative feelings free

- *Write it out*: pour all of your negative thoughts on to the page, then write your way back to positivity again, listing everything you're proud of achieving

- *Meditate*: and visualise your stresses floating away from you

- *Draw a line*: declare that tomorrow is another day and time to start anew

- *Help someone else*: focusing on another's problems is a great way to stop obsessing about your own

To sum it all up, instead of trying so hard to be perfect, celebrate the fact that we're all so perfectly *imperfect*!

What Have You Learnt This Season?

Next week, it will be September. There's a chill in the air now, first and last thing, that brings with it the promise of bonfires, crisp golden leaves and snug woolly jumpers.

But before we bid this beautiful summer au revoir, let's take some time to take stock.

I guess most of us probably sit down at the end of each year to reflect upon the previous twelve months and set goals for the coming year, but why not do the same at the end of each season?

The trouble with limiting ourselves to just new year's resolutions is two-fold.

First of all, they take place in January - officially *The Most Miserable Month of the Year by Miles* - and therefore hardly conducive to happy planning. It is however, massively conducive to giving up at the first hurdle and comfort-eating a herd of Lindt chocolate reindeer.

And secondly, by only sitting down to take stock of our lives once a year, we run the risk of a frenzy of goal-setting for one day, followed by 364 days of drifting aimlessly.

So, in this final week of summer, I invite you to do a little musing with me.

Take a sheet of A4 paper and write at the top:

Things I've Learnt This Summer

Cast your mind back to all of the fun, interesting, silly, random and life-changing events you've experienced these past three months.

Then ask yourself the question: *What have I learnt from each of these things?*

Here's mine to help get you started:

Things I've Learnt This Summer

- ***That the raw pain of loss always eventually passes.*** And once you've worked your way through the darkness, you emerge butterfly-bright into the light. And strong in the knowledge that you never really lose those you've truly loved, as you carry them with you forever in your heart.

- ***That rice cakes contain hidden depths.*** They might look and feel like polystyrene, but once topped with avocado, smoked salmon and a spritz of lemon juice, they become orgasmic. Literally. You know those movies where the shy, bespectacled secretary removes her glasses and shakes loose her hair, revealing that she was actually a smouldering sexpot all along? Well, it turns out rice cakes are the food equivalent.

- ***That Instagram is way too much fun.*** Not only do you have the excitement of never knowing which filter is going to be the winner, it also enables you to transform even the dreariest picture of Auntie Mabel pre-varicose veins op, into a Warhol-esque masterpiece.

- ***That the coastal town of Broadstairs is beautiful.*** Miles of sandy beaches, a second-hand bookstore with a built-in pub, Punch and Judy shows on the bandstand, Morelli's ice-cream parlour and only an hour and twenty minutes from London!

- ***That lying or sitting in stillness can be incredibly productive.*** Creativity needs time and space to incubate, so don't be afraid to do nothing. Repeat after me: *'Busy-ness can be bad for business.'*

- ***That I'm not a freak for wanting a life with no ties.*** It turns out that I'm actually a 'free range human' and part of a growing tribe. Google *'free-range human'* to see if you're part of it too.

- ***That when I make my career dreams about making others happy, I end up making my own self happier than ever too.*** If you're currently feeling demotivated work-wise, try and see how focusing on helping others can help you too.

- ***That frozen yoghurt is actually quite nice.*** I'd always thought that it was a cheap imitation of ice-cream invented to keep health freaks happy. But it turns out I was wrong. *Fro-yo, fo-sho, mo-fo!*

- ***That I will never be down with the kids.*** And should really stop trying to talk gangsta - especially about frozen yoghurt.

- ***That a daily meditation practice works miracles.*** This summer I have actually managed to meditate every single day without fail. I now waft through life like camomile tea in human form. Most days, anyway.

- ***That if you live your life by just this one quote, you won't go far wrong:*** 'Just be good and do good.' Swami Sivanandaji

I hope my list has inspired you to write your own. And when you've finished reflecting on the lessons you've learnt this summer, take a moment to cast your mind forward to the autumn. What would you like to have learnt by the time you're carving out your Halloween pumpkin?

Me, I'd like to:

- Learn to make a Hummingbird cake with salted-caramel frosting.

- Learn how to mount an effective anti-bullying campaign.

- Learn how to film a video without giggling or saying 'er' all the time.

- And learn how to dance the tango!

Have fun compiling your own lessons and don't forget to dare to dream.

The Loneliness of the Long-Distance Dreamer

"All big men are dreamers. They see things in the soft haze of a spring day or in the red fire of a long winter's evening. Some of us let these great dreams die, but others nourish and protect them; nurse them through bad days till they bring them to the sunshine and light, which comes always to those who sincerely hope that their dreams will come true."
Woodrow T. Wilson

So, you have a dream.

A truly magnificent dream.

One that, if and when it comes true, will fill your life with joy.

But the trouble is, because it's so magnificent, it's not the kind of dream to come true overnight.

Or even next week.

Or next month.

This dream is going to be a *long* time in the making.

Maybe it's to set up a new business.

Or to write a screenplay.

Or to emigrate.

How do you maintain the burning passion you felt when you first kindled the dream?

How do you get through the day-to-day drudgery of waiting on your dream, without letting that drudgery make you give up?

Welcome to the loneliness of the long distance dreamer!

Over the past few years, I've been lucky enough to achieve several 'long distance dreams' - just think of me as the Mo Farrah of the dream world - and now I'm going to share my *Top Tips for Staying the Distance.*

- **Create a Dream Board**: I can't emphasise enough the power of visualisation when it comes to your dreams. Creating a visual representation of your dreams helps keep you focused and can act as a powerful reminder if you do start to waver. Fill your board with images and words that will keep you inspired and place it somewhere you will see it every day. Spend regular time in front of your board, drinking in the images and basking in the feelings of excitement and happiness they generate.

- **Take a 'Dream Action Step' every day**: It doesn't matter how small it is, but make it your practise to take one action step towards your dream every day. Regular baby-steps soon build a powerful momentum and it is incredible what can be achieved just by following this simple rule of thumb. Jack Canfield, creator of the best-selling *Chicken Soup for the Soul* books credits his phenomenal success with taking five action steps towards his goal every day - transforming him from a self-published author to an international literary sensation.

- **Feel grateful for your current life**: This is probably the hardest of all the steps. There have been many times when I've been consumed with frustration while I've been waiting for a dream to manifest. It could be that your day job has you going out of your mind with boredom. *I shouldn't be here,* you wail to yourself. *I should be achieving greatness, not having irate* *customers yell at me because they've found a severed thumb in their frozen peas!* (You really have no idea of the hardships I had to endure before becoming a writer...) But the trouble is, if we start wallowing in self-pity and frustration, it brings us down and then we can feel that same sense of lethargy when it comes to our dreams. And then we're less likely to take action to achieve them. So make a list of all that you are grateful for when it comes to your current situation ie; what it has taught you, how it can help you to achieve your dreams and how you have benefited from the experience. The positivity this generates can then be used as fuel for your dreams.

- ***Find a dream theme tune:*** Sportsmen and women often have songs that they play before they compete. Songs that motivate them and get them fired up for success. As a long distance dreamer it's imperative that you find your own dream theme tune - one that will pick you up when the going gets tough and get you re-inspired.

- ***Find a dream mentor:*** Another great way of keeping inspired is to find someone who has already achieved your dream - or something close to it - and learn all about how they did it. Back when my dream was to relaunch my writing career as a Young Adult novelist, I used Jack Canfield as my dream mentor. I read all about how he had used self-publishing as a stepping stone to success and I modelled his methods. I self-published my first YA novel, *Dear Dylan* and took action steps every day to try and make it a success. These steps included sending it to reviewers on both sides of the Atlantic and entering it for a national book award. It went on to win the award, and win me book deals in the UK, France and Germany - exceeding my wildest dreams.

And that is the greatest thing about being a long distance dreamer.

If you keep the faith...

Keep taking baby-steps towards your dreams...

One day you will realise that you've travelled an entire world.

And that what you had dreamed possible was only a fraction of what you ended up creating.

So keep your dreams big and bold and brave.

Keep the faith.

Keep inspired.

Keep taking those baby-steps.

And who knows where they might lead...

10 Ways to Satisfy Your Wanderlust - Without Making Your Wallet Weep

I don't know about you, but the minute summer arrives I get a serious attack of wanderlust.

And I don't know about you, but with all things financial being pretty tight right now, it's a lust that isn't being satisfied.

Until...

dramatic drum roll

...I realised that actually, you don't have to physically wander to satisfy the lust. You can recreate the exact same feelings, vicariously.

Just think of this post as a pulsating piece of travel porn.

And so, without further ado, here are my top ten ways to satisfy your wanderlust, without making your wallet weep...

#1: *See your home town through the eyes of a traveller*
I've lived in London for a large chunk of my life and yet it was only when friends or relatives from overseas came to visit that I actually got to discover its real treasures. It's so easy to get stuck in a familiarity loop between home, work and the same old pubs / restaurants. And we all know what familiarity breeds, right? So get out your Google maps and go and unearth the hidden treasures of your home town.

#2: *Visit a museum or art gallery*
Travel is all about broadening the mind, so broaden yours with a museum trip. Even better - go to a museum or exhibition that you would never normally choose. Mosey on out of your comfort zone to learn all about the Cubist movement or how they

removed the brains from mummies in ancient Egypt. You'll be surprised at how energising this can be.

#3: *Take a trip to your local library*
In these days of government cutbacks, *finding* your local library could be a quest enough in itself. But once you do, set your compass for the Travel Section and peruse the *Lonely Planets* and *Rough Guides.* Pick out books on three places you would love to go to, plus one wild card - Azerbaijan anyone? Read all about the best bars and cheapest cuisine in your dream locations. Positively wallow in the detail. Think of this as a reconnaissance mission before you embark upon the real deal. And speaking of which...

#4: *Set up an official Wanderlust Savings Account*
Even if you can only afford to put in £10 a month - it's a start. And at least you will feel as if the wheels on your travel wagon are in motion.

#5: *Give your old holiday pics an Instagram makeover*
Trawling through old holiday pics and giving them a sun-kissed Instagram glow is a great way of reliving old memories and recapturing the fun and freedom you felt when you took the pic.

#6: *Eat like a traveller*
And no, I don't mean egg and chips from a laminated menu, Magaluf stylie. Give your home-cooking a foreign twist and take your taste buds on a word tour. Seriously people, what are you waiting for? Go fry some plantain!

#7: *Write a future postcard or travel journal entry*
I'm a firm believer in the power of writing when it comes to manifesting your dreams. There's some kind of weird magic that sets to work when you put pen to paper, or fingertip to keyboard, and start writing about your dreams. So write an imaginary postcard or journal entry from your dream destination.

Use any details you may have gleaned from your library expedition in #3 on this list to add real richness and depth to your words. Write until you feel as if you've actually been there. And trust that one day you really will.

#8: *Immerse yourself in travel memoirs*
When you read a well-written travel memoir it's as if the author has stowed you away in their backpack with them. Search for travel memoirs on Amazon and take your pick. The literary world is literally your oyster.

#9: *Have a holiday romance*
No good travel adventure would be complete without a sun-cream scented kiss or two. But you can still have a holiday romance without going on holiday. How? By seeking out a holiday-maker on your own home turf and becoming *their* holiday romance. This might be a bit easier to do if you live in London rather than say, Sizewell (is there such a thing as a nuclear tourist?) but it's got to be worth a shot, right? And is there anything more liberating and exciting than a fleeting moment of passion with a brooding Italian or sultry Spaniard...? (*Top Tip: there are loads in Leicester Square right now.*)

#10: *Adopt a traveller state of mind*
There's no denying it - travelling brings out the adventuresome spirit in most people. And of course, just by adopting a fun-loving, free-styling attitude, you automatically attract more excitement and joy into your life. So right here, right now, make a pact with yourself that for the rest of the summer, you are going to channel Ranulph Fiennes and see the potential for adventure in your everyday routine. Take a different route to work. Get off the bus or train at a random stop.Talk to strangers (*but not in a restraining-order way*). Ask friends to tell you something about them you don't already know – and would be intrigued to discover. See the magical potential for adventure in every moment. Bon voyage, Dare to Dreamers!

Cultivate an Attitude of Gratitude

'If you want to find happiness, find gratitude.' **Steve Maraboli**

This Saturday is World Gratitude Day. World Gratitude Day was initiated in 1977 by the United Nations Meditation Group. The aim of this day of celebrating gratitude is this:

"a holiday for all peoples, a day of meditation for all religions, a day of celebration for all humanity, united by knowledge of simultaneously shared emotion, a day when triumph of the spirit can make a world community."

Personally, I think every day should be World Gratitude Day.

In all of my years as a life coach - and as a human being - gratitude is the one thing that *always* makes me happy.

Always.

Ten years ago, I hit a low point in my life. My marriage had ended in such an extreme and destructive way I felt as if I was trapped in some kind of emotional ground zero.

I didn't just need to rebuild my life, I needed to rebuild *myself*.

I read many different self-help books back in those dark days but in the end the thing that saved me was one simple daily exercise that took just a couple of minutes to complete.

This exercise was keeping a gratitude journal.

Every night, before I went to bed, I would reflect on my day and write down five things that I felt grateful for.

At first it was hard finding *one*.

But I kept on plugging away and soon something really great happened.

Instead of waiting until the end of the day to try and recollect things to be grateful for, I'd start noticing them as they happened.

I'd have a cup of rich blend coffee and a slice of home-made cake and think to myself: *here's something for my list tonight.* Or I'd see a beautiful sunset and make a mental note to remember it later.

Doing the exercise was causing my brain to rewire itself and instead of dwelling on negatives from my past, it was seeking out positives in my present.

Adopting an attitude of gratitude made me view the world through rose-tinted glasses.

And it made me feel happy in the moment.

As I picked my way through the rubble of my break-up, I started seeing glimmers of hope everywhere.

And today, whenever I experience a problem - an argument with another person, a work setback, financial worries - I switch my attitude to gratitude and straight away, I'm back in a place of love and positivity rather than stress and fear.

Give it a try...

Take a moment to think about something or someone who's really pressing your buttons.

Feel the tension in your body as you think about the stress this situation is causing you.

Notice your mind being flooded with fearful thoughts.

Now ask yourself, *what can I feel grateful for in this situation?*

How is this person or issue a blessing?

Please don't curse, I'm being deadly serious. If you think hard enough and look long enough you will be able to find something.

Write your answers down.

And notice any changes in your body and mood as you do so.

Hopefully, your tension should be easing and your mind calming.

Gratitude is a happy pill we can take at any time, in any situation - without prescription.

In the spirit of World Gratitude Day - and to give yourself an instant happiness fix - why don't you join me?

What five things are you grateful for today?

Jot them down in a pad.

Try doing this exercise every day for a couple of weeks and see how it changes your outlook on the world.

Wishing you a blessed time, crammed full of opportunities for gratitude.

Learn From Autumn and Learn to Let Go

Of all the seasons, I believe autumn has the most to teach us.

Oh I know that everyone loves using spring as an opportunity to wax lyrical about life - talking about *new* beginnings and *fresh* starts, and getting all duster-happy in a fit of *spring* cleaning. But today I'd like to make the case for spring's less fresh-faced and perky seasonal sibling - autumn.

Autumn is the season of letting go.

The season of out with the old.

And there are few things healthier in life than letting go of what no longer serves us.

But what is it about us humans that makes us so love to cling on to things that are way past their 'best before' date?

That ink-stained Snoopy sweatshirt we know we'll never wear again.

That book on 100 Ways to Bake a Kumquat *that we know we'll never read.*

Those so-called friendships that leave us drained ... of ... the ... will ... to ... live.

Those fearful thought-patterns that leave us half-crazed.

Those relationships that feel like leaden strait-jackets.

They are stale. Clogging. Sapping.

We need to learn to let go of them all.

And we need to let autumn be our teacher.

You never see a tree clinging to its dying leaves, wailing, *'Oh but it's such a perfect shade of brown!'* Or, *'What if I never grow another one, like ever again?!!'*

A tree in autumn just lets its old leaves drop, safe in the knowledge that some greener, fresher, lovelier ones will come along soon enough.

To make room for the exciting new opportunities in our lives we have to let go of what's dying and dead.
We have to de-clutter our living and work spaces.

We have to clean out our closets.

All those negative thoughts that you plague yourself with?

They're dead thoughts, they do nothing to improve your quality of life, so picture them falling away.

Those friendships or relationships that leave you feeling hurt or frustrated or drained?

Let them go, with love.

An exercise in letting go:

- Play a piece of up-beat music.
- Imagine that you're a tree in a storm.
- Your arms are your branches and they're being blown about in the wind.
- As you shake your arms, visualise all the thoughts and situations and people that you want to be free of, literally being shaken from your life like autumnal leaves.
- Shake them wildly, from every part of your body.

Something wonderful happens when you let go of all the dead things in your life.

You make space for new things and new thoughts and new people that will reignite and re-inspire you.

And you will expand into that space lighter and freer and more joyful than ever.

How to Turn Unexpected Losses into Unexpected Gains

Last week, I had one of those *stop-the-world-I-want-to-get-off* moments.

I found out that I'm probably going to lose my main source of income in the new year.

And I'm having to take a substantial cut in income straight away.

As this is sadly an all too common occurrence in this seemingly never-ending recession, I wanted to share the lessons I've learnt over the past few days.

I think they're pretty universal when it comes to dealing with sudden and dramatic loss. And hopefully they offer a more positive take on what can at first seem catastrophic.

Step One: *Mourn the loss*

If you don't it will come back to haunt you. So allow yourself to feel sad. Allow yourself to cry. Don't even attempt to 'look on the bright side' until you have fully processed the dark side.

Step Two: *Allow your anger*

Loss of anything, be it a job, relationship, friendship or home, is crap. And it is especially crap if you didn't see it coming. You are allowed to feel angry about this. And you should. But make sure you channel your anger in healthy ways. Go for a long hike or run. Do a few rounds of air-boxing - or real boxing if you are able! When you are out driving (preferably along a non-busy road) turn the music up loud and yell your head off. Do an angry dance. Write an angry, sweary letter - *but don't send it!* Get it all out and then...

Step Three: *Feel the fear*

Loss is scary. There you were tootling along on the journey of life and *BAM!* it hits you. Now nothing is going to be the same again. And this inevitably makes you frightened. Oh, how you long for the security of your comfort zone. Oh, how you hate the sudden uncertainty. But fear isn't all bad. If used wisely, fear can be the most effective butt-kicker known to man. Here's how...

Step Four: *Let your fear fire you up*

Take all of the nervous energy swarming around your body and use it as fuel for something more positive.

Step Five: *Dig for the positive*

If you are really honest with yourself, what are you actually quite happy to have lost? What freedom does your brave new world now present you with? What opportunities are now available to you that weren't, pre-loss? In what ways can you turn this situation to your advantage? In what ways can this loss actually lead to your life becoming even better than before?

Step Six: *Act now*

Once you've figured out the ways in which this loss can actually be an opportunity to gain, take IMMEDIATE ACTION to make this happen. One of the worst things about loss is the sense of powerlessness that it creates. By taking action you are reclaiming control of your life and this instantly makes you feel better.

Over the past few days, I've done all of the above.

I've walked around in a state of shock.

I've cried into my pillow.

I've had a bit of a rant and rage.

I've been overcome by a wave of fear.

And then I got my butt back in gear.

I started to see the opportunities that my loss was presenting me with.

The opportunity to quit the dreaded London commute.

The opportunity to spend more time writing books.

And the opportunity to finally realise a dream that I've had bubbling away on the back-burner for years.

I'd been putting it off before because I hadn't got the time or I wasn't quite ready.

But one of the biggest and best lessons I've learnt this past week is that sometimes you have to go for your dreams *before* you are ready.

And when you do, something magical happens.

Anger turns to hope.

Sorrow turns to joy.

Fear turns to courage.

And loss turns to gain.

Until next time, always remember to dare to dream.

Even in the midst of loss. *Especially* in the midst of loss.

Feeling Grateful for the Bad Stuff

Most times
I am a dancing daisy of a soul
Bobbing and smiling
In Love's gentle breeze

But sometimes
Some Times
I feel the weight of the world
On my working mum's shoulders

Some Times
All I see are
Bills and stress and
Re...spon...si...bil...ity

Some Times
I feel fatigue
Seeping into my bones
Heavy as lead

Some Times
I want to drop
To the floor
And weep

But those times
Those Times
I stop the world
And I get off

And I walk
A walk of thanks
Every step
Celebrating a gift

My son
My home
My family
My friends

Thank you
Thank you
Thank you
Thank you

The evening birdsong
The sweet coiling wood smoke
The rain's silver shimmer
Thank you.

The beat of my heart
The song of my dreams
The feet marching me back to the dance
Thank you.

Welcome Pain and Fear - and Watch Them Dissolve

When pain or fear come calling, our first instinct is to tense.

Our bodies tighten and our minds fill with negative chatter.

And what we resist

persists

and persists

and persists.

As we struggle with our unwelcome guests they become bigger.

And we feel smaller.

And as we feel smaller, other unwelcome thoughts and feelings start crowding in.

'We heard you were throwing a panic party and we'd like to join you!'

And now they're coming at you from all sides, these negative thoughts and jittery feelings.

What do you do?

How do you get rid of them?

How do you stop yourself from drowning?

Here's how.

Simply STOP.

Stop struggling.

Stop fearing.

Stop fighting these feelings.

Sit openly in stillness.

And welcome them in.

Welcome them in.

Breathe slowly and calmly.

In through the nose.

And out through the mouth.

And keep silently repeating the mantra: *'It's OK.'*

Because it is OK.

It's OK to feel pain.

It's OK to feel fear.

And as soon as you acknowledge them...

Allow them...

And accept them...

They start to disappear.

Dissolving back into Love. Into calm. Into peace.

The 3 Questions That Guarantee Happiness

In all the years I've been coaching, there are three questions that never fail to bring a smile to a client's face.

So I've decided to share these *happy-pills-in-question-form* to spread the joy.

Take some time out to answer them, *writing your answers down* so that they really register, and I guarantee you'll come away feeling heaps better.

Question One: *What ten things are you most proud of achieving?*

If you can list more than ten, then go right ahead. The more is definitely the merrier as far as this question goes!

Question Two: *What did you love to do as a child?*

What imaginary games or friends did you create? Where did you like to play? And with who? What were your favourite childhood stories and TV shows? What were your favourite sweets? Who was your favourite super-hero? Don't rush this trip down Memory Lane, really revel in it, recalling all the details.

Question Three: *What are your greatest dreams?*

How would you like your home-life, work-life and personal-life to look, this time next year? Write about them in as much detail as possible and really imagine them coming true - and how that would make you feel.

Sometimes you need to take a moment out of life's hustle and bustle to sit back and take stock.

You need to be proud of your achievements.

You need to let your inner child out to play.

You need to let your dreams be your guide.

By taking the time to regularly answer these three questions you'll keep yourself rooted in happiness - and what better way to live?

Winter Solstice Thanks

The winter solstice is approaching. The shortest day. The longest night. Traditionally, a time to pause, take stock and give thanks.

Although most winter solstice traditions have been lost in the crazed consumer fest of Christmas, I think we could all benefit from following the winter sun's example at this time of year as it appears to stand still in the sky.

Stop.

Reflect.

Appreciate.

Let go.

Then we're able to move into the new year, optimistic and baggage-free.

One of the most effective ways of achieving this is to write the closing year a thank you letter.

Take some time when you won't be interrupted. Play some soothing music.

And begin to write:

Dear 20XX,

Thank you for . . .

Give thanks for the people who have brought light into your life this year.

The people who have enriched you, made you laugh, love and learn.

Give thanks for all the opportunities you have been given in your work or education.

Give thanks for your home.

And for all the places you got to see this year.

Give thanks for those magical, memorable moments that have been sprinkled throughout the past twelve months: the intimate moments, the unforgettable conversations, the incredible insights. Treasure them all, with your words of thanks.

Give thanks for your health - and if this year has seen your health suffer, give thanks for the positive things that have come from this (you will find some, if you dig hard enough).

And now for the 'fun' part - give thanks to everyone and everything that has caused you pain.

Thank them for the lessons they have taught you; the opportunities to practise understanding and forgiveness. The opportunity to love unconditionally.

Say *'thank you'* and then, *'no more, thank you'*.

End your letter of thanks to the year by detailing all those people, situations and patterns of behaviour that no longer serve you.

Before the year ends, let them go, with love and thanks.

Then sit for a while.

In stillness.

And see the coming year stretching before you.

A blank canvas.

Awaiting your most colourful dreams...

The Pressure of Pretty

Imagine a world where women and girls weren't celebrated for how they look but for what they do.

Imagine a world where magazine headlines shouted stories of achievement and kindness instead of body image and sex.

Imagine a world where girls weren't starving themselves, harming themselves and crying themselves to sleep because of the pressure on them to be 'pretty'.

Imagine a world where 60% of women didn't end up hating their bodies.

When I was writing my book *True Face* I asked young women to contact me with their stories of how they'd been affected by this pressure.

Some of the emails I received moved me to tears.

There were stories of girls as young as fourteen skipping meals, consuming nothing but diet drinks, eating *nothing solid*, because they were ashamed of being a Size 10 or 12.

I can remember a time when being a Size 12 was considered slim.

But then some joker invented Size Zero - with the implication that to achieve the perfect body, you literally had to waste away to nothing.

And it's not enough to slim down to zero - everywhere we look we are bombarded with images of 'pretty'.

Images that, more often than not, are achieved only with the help of an airbrush or a surgeon's knife.

'*Because you're worth it*,' the shampoo slogan reassures - right next to a vision of unattainable perfection guaranteed to make most of us feel *worthless*.

From the pinch-waisted princesses we're supposed to aspire to as children, to the swollen-chested, stick-thin celebrities we aspire to as adults, we've been brainwashed into thinking that image is all.

Pretty is our mantra.

It is also our curse.

It inspires mass insecurity, jealousy and fear.

If a woman dares to talk about being pretty, she can almost certainly expect a bitter backlash from other women. Just ask the UK journalist Samantha Brick, who received a torrent of abuse - including death threats - when she wrote an article on the subject.

Hers might be an extreme example but who hasn't gathered around a PC in the office to dissect a celebrity's figure, clothes or looks?

Who hasn't immediately scanned another woman's outfit, make-up and hair when she walks into the room?

And if that woman is stunningly beautiful, who doesn't feel a wistful twinge at best and a jealous stab at worst?

When I lost some weight a few years ago I can remember a couple of other women making snide remarks. One of them even asked me if I had an eating disorder.

To put this into some kind of context, I never dropped below a Size 10.

And this to me, is the real tragedy when it comes to the pressure of pretty.

Instead of uniting and saying enough of this crap, we've been so blinded by the crap that we start turning on each other. Looking at thin women with envy, and overweight women with smug contempt.

This is not our natural state.

We aren't born with eating disorders or suffering from self-loathing.

As babies, we don't point to our nappies and say, *'Does my bum look big in this?'*

As young children, we don't think, *'oh if only my hair had more volume and shine'* when playing with our friends.

We're too busy enjoying ourselves!

But now girls as young as seven are being admitted to hospital with anorexia.

Girls as young as seven are starving themselves to death.

Girls as young as thirteen are dreaming of plastic surgery.

Women and girls of all ages are trapped in a never-ending cycle of vanity and self-loathing.

Isn't it time we said, *enough is enough*?

Isn't it time we demanded more from our magazines and media?

Isn't it time we realised that 'pretty' isn't the least bit empowering?

Pretty is insipid and silly and doesn't really mean a thing.

Our lives are so precious. And so, so short.

Let's not waste them obsessing over calories, or pouting for endless selfies, or bitching about others.

Let's make something of ourselves and our time here.

Let's make a real and lasting difference.

And let's start by taking a stand.

Reboot Your Way to Happiness

Have you ever had one of those days where everything - and I mean EVERYTHING - goes wrong?

Your alarm clock fails to go off.

There's no hot water for a shower.

You ladder your tights in your rush to get dressed (boys, insert the male equivalent - snag your y-fronts maybe...?)

Your train to work is late.

While you wait - *in the rain* - you decide to check Facebook and discover that your ex is now dating a supermodel look-alike, your friend Smuggy McStatus is 'sooooo happy' on her tenth holiday of the year and your other friend Humble McBraggy has just been promoted - *again*.

By the time the train arrives it's packed to the rafters, stinks of 'morning breath' and you're travelling under your own personal thought-bubble of gloom.

This day. My life. The entire world. SUCKS.

Well, stop right there.

All you need to do to prevent the descent into The Official Day from Hell is to give yourself a reboot.

And how do you do that?

Simple.

Close your eyes.

Just like when you reboot a computer, imagine yourself shutting down.

Focus on your breathing, to switch off your thoughts.

In through the nose: *one ... two ... three.*

Out through the mouth: *three ... two ... one.*

Repeat this process until you feel your body relax.

As you do so, picture all of the things that have stressed you out, floating away like balloons on the breeze.

Higher and higher.

And further and further.

Until they're just specks in your distant memory.

Then begin to reboot.

Think of ten things that you are grateful for, right here, right now.

If you get to ten and can think of more, keep going.

Feel your happy-self starting to whir back into life.

Pick up the momentum by thinking of someone you really, truly love.

Someone who makes your life gloriously simple and your heart do nothing but smile.

Then, to complete the rebooting process, think of one loving thing you're going to do today.

One random act of kindness that will cause another person joy.

See how the act of bringing joy is completely and wondrously reciprocal, as the mere thought causes joy to surge into you.

Reboot complete.

You're welcome :)

How to Begin a Brand New Chapter in Your Life Story

Sometimes, we just need to draw a line in our lives, marking the end so that we can embrace the new.

It could be following a relationship break-up, or leaving a job, or maybe just a joyless period of time that you'd be glad to see the back of.

A great way of doing this is to view your life as a story, with you as the writer as well as the hero.

If your life were a story, how could you make the next chapter one to remember - for all the right reasons?

How could you make this the chapter in which our hero - *you* - has the most fun, brings the most love and lives their - *your* - life to the fullest?

In journalism they say a story isn't complete unless you answer the five Ws and one H:

Who?
What?
When?
Where?
Why?
How?

So, let's apply this rule to your life's new chapter.

Grab a notebook and pen.

Put on some soulful music.

And free-write away to your heart's content.

Who...

... do you want to spend more time with?
... do you need to forgive in order to move forward?
... do you need to let go of, with love?

What...

... are you most grateful for?
... are your wildest dreams?
... are the steps you can take towards achieving these dreams?
... are the limiting beliefs you need to let go of in order to achieve them?

When...

... can you realistically achieve your goals by?
... can you make more time for yourself?
... can you make more time for fun?

Where...

... do you want to go?
... makes you feel happy and free?
... would you like to be by this time next year?

Why...

... is this next chapter important to you?
... do you deserve to have a great time?
... do you need to stop being hard on yourself?

How...

... can you be true to yourself?
... can you be your brightest, most loving self?
... can you make this your best chapter yet?

Wishing you all a brand new chapter, crammed full of fun, happiness, adventure and love.

The Secret Formula for a Great Life

Sometimes when I'm running a writing workshop, I share this formula for a great story:

Character + Dream + Obstacles + Determination & Imagination = Great Story

The fact is, if the lead character in a story has no dreams or goals, there's no excitement.

If they have no obstacles standing in the way of them achieving their goals, there's no drama.

And if they have no determination and imagination, they won't be able to overcome their obstacles and there'll be no satisfactory outcome.

Today, I'd like you to apply that formula to your own life:

You + Dream + Obstacles + Determination & Imagination = Great Life Story

The fact is, life is one long obstacle course.

And if we don't have the determination and imagination needed to overcome the obstacles we're presented with, we stop being the writers of our own life stories.

We let doubt and fear dictate the course of our lives instead.

And we end up deeply unhappy.

Many years ago, as I know I've already told you (my therapist says if I keep sharing it will eventually lessen the trauma!), I worked in the complaints department for a chain store.

All day long, I had to deal with ranty phone calls and letters from irate customers.

It was miles away from my **dream** job of being a novelist.

One day, when a customer sent me the dead cockroach they'd found in their ice-cream taped to their letter, I decided that enough was enough.

I became *determined* that I would achieve my goal and get paid for writing books instead of grovelling apology letters for 'Cockroach Surprise' ice-cream.

Then I used my *imagination* to figure out how I could do that, deciding to teach myself how to write and to approach writing like any other business, starting off with short stories and articles and working my way up to a book.

What is your dream?

What are you determined to change in your life?

What obstacles are you determined to overcome?

Imagine for a moment that you're a character in a movie or novel.

If you were writing this character's story, how would you get them to overcome their obstacles with determination and imagination?

What would make for an exciting and inspiring story?

What decisions and actions would have audiences or readers cheering your character on?

Free-write your ideas in a notebook.

Viewing your life as a story and yourself as the writer can be a great way to circumnavigate your self-doubt and fear.

Whether you have any literary ambitions or not, never forget that there's one story you're constantly creating; your own life story.

Make it great.

Make it inspiring.

Make it *un-put-downable*.

All it takes is imagination and determination.

Smiley-Face Your World

Picture the scene.

I'm on a train into London.

It's the rush hour - aka the *crush* hour.

The man sitting next to me has fallen asleep on my shoulder.

The woman standing next to me has positioned her butt two inches from my face. With every sway of the train, her butt threatens to smother me.

Behind me, a woman is busy telling the train how important she is via a bellowed conversation on her mobile phone.

'I have a meeting at the BBC at ten ... Tell Dominic I've sent the script over...'

The heating is on full pelt. But there's no room to take your coat off. There's no room to move. Period.

I'm on my way to a work meeting that's making me feel as deflated as a Christmas balloon in June.

My Kindle's run out of juice.

I have nothing to look at but butt.

The train grinds to a halt.

The guard utters the two words every commuter dreads: '*signal failure*.'

The carriage slumps into a collective despair.

My phone rings.

It's a teacher from my son's school.

She wants to know why he's late in.

She talks to me like I'm a five-year-old in need of a naughty step.

Something inside of me snaps.

Weeks of unexpressed tension bubble up inside of me.

I switch off my phone and close my eyes.

Something is wrong.

Something in my life is off-kilter.

It's not just Monday morning being its usual evil self.

It's bigger than that.

But what?

I wait for guidance.

It comes quickly.

Write two lists, it says.

One of all the things in your life that make you happy.

One of all the things in your life that make you sad.

I nudge the sleeping man from my shoulder and take my notepad from my bag.

I draw two columns.

One headed with a smiley face and one with a frown.

The smiley column soon fills with all the things in my life that make me come alive.

Dancing, walking, being in nature, travelling, writing from the heart, blogging, coaching, public speaking, friends and loved ones, good food, great company.

There are only three things in the frowny column.

Three things that have to go.

I close my eyes and picture my life free from these soul-sappers.

I start to smile.

I think of how, in the next few months, I can phase them out.

My smile grows even bigger.

I picture a life that's one big smiley-faced column.

I contemplate the decisions and the risks and the out and out courage it will take to make that happen.

I feel really frickin' excited.

The train judders back into life.

The man next to me grunts.

The butt in front of me strays perilously close.

The bellowy-voiced woman behind me loses her signal.

I keep on grinning at the sweet simplicity of it all.

Sometimes you just need to see your life in two columns - one smiley, one sad - in order to figure out what needs to be done; what you need to treasure and what you need to cull.

I arrive in London a walking, talking, smiley-face, with a head full of dreams and an imagination sparking with new ideas.

Now it's your turn.

Write two lists.

One of all the things in your life that make you happy.

One of all the things in your life that make you sad.

Dear Dare to Dream: When Will I Stop Obsessing About My Weight?

Dear Dare to Dream,

Ever since I can remember, I've been obsessed about my weight.

I don't have an eating disorder but I'm almost constantly thinking about food and watching what I eat.

If I think I've eaten too much I punish myself by skipping a meal or working out really hard. I would definitely describe my relationship to food as love hate. I love the feeling of comfort it gives me when I pig out on bread and cheese or chocolate. But I hate myself afterwards.

I'm a Size 14 so I know I'm not huge but some days I really feel like it and I'll look at myself in the mirror and feel really sick at the size of my stomach or the roll of fat at the top of my thighs.

My dream is to be free from this love hate relationship with food. But I've had it ever since I was a teen so I'm not sure if it's even possible.

How and when can I stop obsessing about my weight?

love,

Stress Head x

Dear Stress Head,

The short answer to your question is:

When you love yourself enough.

When you love yourself enough you will stop obsessing about your weight.

But this is a highly complex subject and an issue that's been plaguing you for years by the sounds of it and short answers just won't do.

So, here's my long answer:

I wonder how many millions of women all over the planet can relate to your statement: *'I don't have an eating disorder but...'*

I know I can.

I know I've had many moments of self-loathing when I've looked in the mirror.

I know I've seen images of supermodels and sighed with despair at their concave stomachs and stick-thin limbs.

I know I've tucked into many a chocolate cake and had the deliciousness of the experience soured with feelings of guilt.

But I also now know that the images we're fed by the fashion industry and the media are - to borrow a favourite phrase of my dad's - *'a load of old bollocks'*.

It's all so unfair: we're constantly being told we should look a certain way and yet, short of starvation, or the ability to air-brush our actual bodies, it's impossible to achieve.

Kate Moss was once quoted as saying: *'Nothing tastes as good as skinny feels.'*

Oh really, Kate Moss? Well, why don't you get on a plane to Africa and tell that to one of the 805 million people on the planet who don't have enough to eat?

And that is the devastating irony about this situation: ***one in nine people on this planet don't have enough to eat, while the rest of us are being fed the bullshit that having the body of a starvation victim is somehow cool.***

I've lost track of the number of times I've been out with women - intelligent women, lovely women, women with so much to offer the world, *slim* women - and the conversation has turned to body image and these women have morphed into wailing wimps.

'I feel so over-weight!'

'I have to give up eating sugar / wheat / dairy!'

'My stomach is so bloated!'

'Do I look fat in this?'

And, as the author of several young adult novels, I've received countless emails from teenage girls about the pressures on them to be thin.

Emails from 14-year-olds telling me they regularly go without meals so they can lose weight.

Heart-breaking.

So, dear *Stress Head*, we are starting from a massive disadvantage when it comes to body image and food as we have entire industries intent on making us feel bad about ourselves.

But, taking the fashion industry and media out of the equation for a moment, let's focus on you.

You talk about finding comfort in food.

Does this comfort go deeper than simple enjoyment?

Do you seek solace in food at times of stress?

Many people do. And it certainly isn't a crime.

But, if it makes you unhappy; if you know that in these times you're eating to an unhealthy excess, then you need to look at finding your comfort elsewhere.

The best place I can think to start is in a journal.

The next time the crap hits the fan and you find yourself reaching for the cheese board, pick up a notebook and pen instead.

Free-write about your feelings. Let it all flow. Don't worry about spellings or grammar or any of that stuff. Just get all of your stress out on to the page.

Then write about how you might change your situation for the better.

Ask yourself where the opportunity to love is, in particular, ask: *where is the opportunity to love myself?*

Finish by writing down five things you are grateful for.

By doing this you will hopefully defuse the trigger feelings and your desire to overeat.

I began my reply to you by saying that when you love yourself enough, you will stop obsessing about your weight.

And it's true.

Self-love forms a much-needed barrier against all the images we're fed by the media.

It stops us wanting to starve or 'punish' ourselves.

When we hear some eejit say *'nothing tastes as good as skinny feels'* it makes us want to shove a cheesecake in their gob, rather than rush to the nearest bathroom to make ourselves sick.

Self-love makes us want to live our best lives and create and adventure and love to the max.

And it makes us want to fill our bodies with the nutrients necessary to do that.

So, dear Stress Head, write a list, right now, of all the reasons you're entirely loveable.

All the things you're proud of achieving and creating.

All the people you've helped.

All the love you've brought to the world.

Take some time to really let this sink in.

Then write a list of all the things you dream of one day achieving.

All of the adventures and the fun times and the work goals and the love.

Take some time visualising these things; living out your dreams in your head.

This is what truly matters.

Not that extra slice of cheese you ate last night, or the size of your thighs.

Your life matters.

Your health matters.

Your happiness matters.

The mark you make on the world matters.

Don't stress any more, Stress Head, enjoy.

Enjoy your life and your health and your food.

I'd like to leave you with a beautiful quote from Anne Frank.

Read it whenever you're feeling a pang of self-loathing when you look in the mirror or after eating.

"Everyone has inside of him a piece of good news. The good news is that you don't know how great you can be! How much you can love! What you can accomplish! And what your potential is."

Read it and believe it.

With love,

Siobhan x

You're Not a F***ing Superhero - and that's OK

Recently, work-stress and personal stress and bill stress and not-getting-paid-on-time stress converged to form a perfect storm in my head.

At exactly that moment, my son happened to say something slightly (and I mean infinitesimally) insensitive and I erupted.

In short, this mama had a meltdown.

And, as I'm prone to do in the midst of a meltdown, I said something stupid. Something that instantly made me feel like a crap human being.

And before I knew it, I was speeding off on the down escalator to doom.

Why did you say that?
Why can't you deal with pressure better?
Why do you put up with being disrespected in work?
Why are you taking your stress out on your kid?
Why are you such a crap mum?

So I did what I always do in times of crisis - I shut myself in the bathroom and had a cry.

And then I did what I always try to remember to do in times of crisis: I prayed to God / my inner wisdom / the Universe / Spirit / Shakti / Shakin' Stevens / or whoever / whatever you might believe in, for guidance.

'Please help me out of this downward spiral,' I pleaded.

Then I waited for some kind of divine inspiration.

'You're not a f***ing super hero . . . and that's OK,' came the almost immediate response. (Please note: I have the kind of God who sometimes swears at me, but only when I truly need it.)

'You're not a f***ing super hero . . . and that's OK.'

I felt the weight of the day beginning to ease.

The two looming book deadlines.

The frustrations of being treated with utter disrespect by someone I'm doing some writing for.

The bills that seem to arrive on a daily basis.

The stress of the constant work/home life juggling act.

None of us are superhuman and yet so often, we place super human expectations upon ourselves.

We expect ourselves to deal with the pressures life can throw at us and still skip along merrily whistling, *What a Beautiful World*.

By reminding ourselves that it's OK to mess up, we instantly relieve the pressure.

I let myself out of the bathroom and went and gave my son a hug.

It turned out he wasn't upset with me at all.

And I was reminded yet again, that the only thing that truly matters is who and how we love.

Climbing a Hill of Hope

Sometimes - *often*times - it's all too easy to get trapped in a downward spiral of negative thoughts.

What if becomes *I can't...*

I wish I could becomes *I'll never...*

And instead of encouraging ourselves, we become our own worst enemy, seeking out reason after reason for everything going wrong.

But there's one sure-fire way of breaking this cycle of gloom (*and I apologise if you're reading this in the plains of Nebraska or on a getaway from it all break in a desert*) - climb a hill.

Several years ago, I went to a workshop run by author Gill Edwards. Towards the end of the workshop, she led us all in a guided meditation where we had to visualise ourselves climbing a mountain.

As we climbed, we also had to picture ourselves discarding our fears one by one.

By the time she'd guided us to the top, I felt a sense of freedom and release so powerful I've never forgotten it.

Recently, when I moved house right next to a very steep hill, I adapted this meditation into a physical exercise. It's been so effective I had to share it with you.

So, dear *Dare to Dreamers*, if you sometimes find yourself drowning in negative thoughts, I heartily recommend you give it a go.

First, find a hill (or a mountain, if you're feel particularly hardcore).

At the foot of the hill, get clear on one of your current negative thoughts, such as:

I'll never make any money

I'm so unhappy

I'll never fall in love

I hate my relationship

Then as you prepare to climb the hill, make it your intention to mentally climb your way out of your negativity and fear.

With every step you take, visualise your old, fearful thoughts being left behind you at the bottom of the hill and climb your way into more positive thoughts.

For example, if your negative thought was: *'I'm always going to be broke'*, picture yourself climbing up to a slightly more positive thought, such as, '*I'm broke at the moment but that could all change soon.*'

Keep climbing, and keep raising the positive vibration of your thoughts too.

'One way I could have more money would be to take on more freelance work / cut my expenses / ask my boss for a rise.'

Keep on climbing as briskly as possible and enjoy the physical sensation of working your way out of your gloom.

'If I really cut down on my out-goings and worked my butt off

for the next couple of months I could actually clear my overdraft.'

Keep on climbing and visualising your fearful, negative thoughts being left behind.

'If my boss doesn't give me a rise I could start looking for a new job.'

Keep your eyes on the top of the hill, work your arms and legs, feel your heartbeat increase, enjoy the sensation of fresh air in your lungs.

'I could type up a new CV as soon as I get home and start looking for jobs on spec. I could sign up with an employment agency, get a feel for what else is out there.'

When you reach the top of the hill, stop.

Take a moment to drink in the view.

Enjoy the feeling of space.

Revel in your new perspective.

Picture your fearful thoughts discarded way below you, as tiny as ants.

Look at the vast expanse of sky and fill it with your new, positive, hopes and dreams.
Take a moment to connect with God, the universe, spirit, your inner self (whatever works for you) and give thanks for all that you do have.

Give thanks also, for your new hope.

Then start your descent, bringing your new-found positivity with you every step of the way.

Save Time and Free Your Mind – By Writing a 'To Don't' List

My name's Siobhan.

And I'm a list-oholic.

For years now, writing lists has been a daily habit of mine.

Shopping lists.

Ideas lists.

Dream lists.

And of course - the big daddy of the list world - *the TO DO list.*

As a very busy, self-employed mum, my TO DO lists devour entire blocks of post-it notes in days.

Writing them helps me maintain some kind of order and the comforting sense that, even though I've got about a million and one things TO DO, it's okay, because I've put them all on a list.

And if they're on a TO DO list, they will be done.

But then I read a great article about saving time by doing less and it really got me thinking.

Could my TO DO lists actually be bad for my productivity levels, not to mention my emotional health?

At first, the thought of kicking my TO DO list habit brought me out in a cold sweat. Yes, some of my TO DO lists are almost as long as my books, but I'm self-employed. I have to say yes to everything, don't I?

Don't I?

And what about the spine-tingling satisfaction the moment you tick the last thing off your list? How could I possibly live without that particular thrill?

But the fact is, as soon as I've ticked off one TO DO list, I'm already starting a new one. The thrill is only ever fleeting.

Then I had a brainwave.

What if I were to write a TO DON'T list instead?

So I sat down with a pad and a pen and thought of all the things that sap my time and energy. All the things that I could actually stop doing and the world wouldn't implode - and here's what I came up with:

MY TO DON'T LIST

- *Don't watch or read things that make your brain shrink*

- *Don't spend so much time online*

- *Don't switch on your social media notifications*

- *Don't say yes to freelance jobs that make your soul shudder - life's way too short*

- *Don't be afraid to follow your true calling*

- *Don't procrastinate - your time is precious, spend it on things that make you come alive*

- *Don't judge or gossip - or anything else that blocks you from your true potential*

- *Don't let other people's fear hold you back*

- *Don't let your own fear hold you back*

- *Don't forget to dance, love and dream*

Writing my TO DON'T list felt great. It was like I was descaling my mind the way you descale a kettle; getting rid of all the habits and things that clog up my life and time.

I will still write TO DO lists, but before I add anything to them, I'm going to test it with these 3 questions:

Is this thing absolutely vital to my well-being?

Will it make me feel fulfilled and alive?

Will it add to the levels of love and happiness in the world?

If the answer is no, it's going straight on my TO DON'T list.

Dealing With Overwhelm – One Stepping Stone at a Time

Next month, I'm moving house.

Last month, a friend of mine died.

So this month, overwhelm has become a bit of a nuisance-caller in my life.

Just as I think I'm on top of things, I realise I've forgotten to organise another thing for the move.

Just as I think I'm feeling happy again, I'm side-swiped by sorrow.

Overwhelm descends and all I can think is *Oh God*.

Oh God, how am I going to get it all done?

Oh God, why did she have to die?

But I'm getting through it.

And I'm getting through it by tackling the overwhelm one stepping stone at a time.

I make one call to book the removal firm. I pack one box. I clear one cupboard.

I don't fight the pain of loss. I take it with me on runs and walks, and to my meditation pillow.

I let it move through me.

And, one stepping stone at a time, I feel myself edging out of overwhelm and into a brighter, happier future.

Dare to Expand into Your Magnificence

"Do not let others create your world for you, for they will always create it too small."
Edwin Louis Cole

Have you ever felt squashed into a job, a relationship, a family, a life, that you've had to shrink yourself to fit?

Have you ever had to silence your voice, stifle your passions and smother your desires in order to keep someone else happy?

Have you ever played small and insignificant for fear of angering or upsetting someone?

Have you ever felt dead inside or eaten up with resentment as a result?

I know I have.

Many times.

I've not spoken my truth for fear of triggering another's anger.

I've not celebrated successes for fear of triggering another's jealousy.

I've not spoken out about injustice for fear of incurring another's hatred.

I've not told a bullying boss to f*** the hell off for fear of losing my job.

In the past, I've silenced my voice and stifled my passions countless times out of fear.

And I've gone through life, a miniature, muted version of the creative, passionate, adventurous human being I truly am.

Today, take a moment to see how you are playing it small out of fear.

Who or what are you allowing to shrink your world, your life, your *you*?

And how can you take steps to reclaim your voice, your passions, your identity?

Life is an expansive and magnificent adventure when you stride forward boldly with courage and love.

Dare to expand into your magnificence.

How Are You Lying to Yourself?

Hello, hello!

Today's post is short and sweet because I'm five weeks into a six week writing deadline and my keyboard is starting to weep.

So, this blog is more of a question (*a blogstion...?*)

Right here, right now, how are you lying to yourself?

The fact is, we usually lie to ourselves WAY more convincingly than we lie to others.

So convincingly in fact, that we often don't even realise we're doing it.

So, if you've been telling yourself that you just aren't good enough / clever enough / attractive enough / *enough* enough, hold that thought and put it to the test.

Ask yourself, is this absolutely, definitely, emphatically true? Can I prove it without a shadow of a doubt?

And if you've been judging someone else for being too this, too that, or too the other, hold that thought and put it to the test.

Ask yourself, is this absolutely, definitely, emphatically true? Can I prove it without a shadow of a doubt?

If the answer is no, then you've been lying to yourself.

But that's okay.

Now it's time to embrace the truth.

Maybe, just maybe, you are good enough / clever enough / attractive enough / *enough* enough.

Maybe, just maybe, that person you've been judging isn't 'too' anything at all.

Telling the truth to yourself brings inner peace, confidence and joy.

Telling the truth to yourself sets you free.

Till next time, with love...

Achieve Your Dreams the 3-a-Day Way

"Follow your bliss and the universe will open doors where there were only walls."
Joseph Campbell

It's easy to dream.

All you have to do is close your eyes and just imagine.

But how do you make those dreams come true?

All too often, doubt and fear can spring up like traps and stop you in your tracks.

I used to be world class at letting fear sabotage my dreams.

Then I discovered the 3-a-day way - and it's no exaggeration to say that it transformed my life.

Several years ago, after having four books for adults traditionally published, I self-published my first novel for young adults, *Dear Dylan*.

As soon as the book was published my Inner Voice of Doom started a running commentary in my head.

No-one will buy it.
Everyone will hate it.
How will anyone even know it exists?
No-one will take a self-published book seriously.

And so, in a bid to over-ride my voice of doom, I decided to do 3 things every day to try and promote the book.

I approached book reviewers.

I offered to write guest blogs.

I ran competitions with the book as the prize.

Obviously, not all of these things came off.

But it's a numbers game. And if you're doing 3 things a day, every day, after a month or so things really start to happen.

After a couple of months, reviews of *Dear Dylan* were popping up all over the place.

Then one day, when I was trying to decide what to do for my 3-a-day, I read an article about submissions for a National Book Award.

Of course, my inner voice of doom immediately started yelling, *'you can't enter a self-published book to a national book award!'*

But, buoyed up by the good reception the book was getting online - and wanting to fulfil my 3-a-day quota - I mailed a copy of *Dear Dylan* to the address on the article.

I will never forget the joy I felt when, several months later, I received an email telling me my book had been short-listed.

And when *Dear Dylan* went on to win the award, it was way beyond any of my wildest dreams.

This is what can happen when we slowly, steadily pursue our dreams, 3 daily steps at a time.

Momentum builds.

Magic happens.

Dear Dylan ended up going to auction and winning me book

deals in several countries.

And yet, the inner battle with self-doubt and fear never goes away.

This week, I published the first novel on my Dare to Dream imprint.

And despite everything that happened with *Dear Dylan*, my inner voice of doom is still going strong.

No-one will buy it.
No-one will like it.
No-one will take it seriously.

But that's OK, because I know exactly what to do.

I'm going to keep on walking towards my dreams, 3 daily steps at a time.

How about you...?

Sickness as a Spiritual Practice

"The goal of spiritual practice is full recovery, and the only thing you need to recover from, is a fractured sense of self."
Marianne Williamson

Last week, I got sick.

Really sick.

Sheet-soaking, fever sick.

Normally, I hate getting ill.

As someone who likes to be on the go all the time and as a self-employed person, I hate anything that confines me to my bed for days on end and causes me to lose valuable income.

But last week, as I started feeling really down about my predicament, it struck me that actually, getting sick is a great opportunity to deepen your spiritual practice.

Or, for those of you who aren't spiritually inclined, *it's a great opportunity for inner peace.*

And here's why:

Sickness brings an opportunity to be here now

All too often we spend our time haunted by or harking back to past experiences, or projecting wistfully or fearfully into an unknown future. The key to inner peace is to be in the present moment. To *really be* in the present moment. When you are sick, you have less distractions.

Instead of pining for the healthier days of the past or future, practise being in the present moment - no matter how snotty, achy or feverish that present moment might be.

Tips for being here now: Simply lie in peace and stillness. If it helps, listen to a guided meditation, there are loads of them on YouTube.

Sickness brings an opportunity for patient acceptance

It's easy to accept life when all is going your way, but if you can accept feeling lousy and relax into your illness you're actually doing your immune system a massive favour. By not fighting your illness emotionally and getting stressed out about it, you are giving your body the best possible chance to heal itself.

Tips for patient acceptance: Watch comedies, devour easy-read novels, listen to chill-out CDs.

Sickness brings an opportunity to let go

In our society we are conditioned to strive for and cling to goals and achievements. The first thoughts that crossed my mind when I got sick last week were, *I can't be ill, I have a book to finish. I have another book to promote. My entire career will go down the toilet if I have any time off right now!* I saw almost instantly that this was a great opportunity to let go of my attachment to my work goals. And so I replaced my crazy thoughts with a far more peaceful alternative; *whatever will be, will be.* Then I put my laptop in a cupboard, cancelled all of my meetings for the week and let go. And it felt great.

Tips for letting go: Hide your laptop, come offline, switch off your phone.

Sickness brings an opportunity to face fear - and see it fade

Illness can often bring with it a huge side-helping of fear. Fear of the consequences of being ill - loss of earnings, undelivered work etc and fear of the illness itself. Although this can be one of the worst aspects of being sick, it also brings the greatest opportunity for inner peace. Learning how to face your fears and see them fade is a super-power when it comes to inner peace. But how do you do this when faced with a serious illness?

Several years ago, I was diagnosed with an auto-immune disease that basically killed off my thyroid gland. It also made me lose loads of hair, feel permanently cold and lethargic and turned me into an emotional wreck. And I was told that it would make me put on a ton of weight. As you can imagine, this diagnosis made me feel extremely fearful, not helped any by my consultant, who told me that there was nothing I could do about it and I'd be on meds for the rest of my life - meds that are linked to high cholesterol and heart disease. I overcame my fear by taking control of my own recovery. I looked up all I could about my disease. I found examples of people who had refused to accept such a bleak diagnosis and I devised my own action plan based on my findings, changing my diet and life-style accordingly. Instantly, my fear began to fade as I no longer felt powerless in the face of my diagnosis. My hair grew back, my energy levels returned, as did my happiness, I didn't put on any excess weight and I've brought my medication levels right down too.

Tips for facing your fear: Know that your health must come first - work can wait. Take control of your recovery.

Sickness brings an opportunity for self-love

In my humble opinion, nothing is more important than Love. And this is especially true when you are sick. There can be the tendency to want to martyr ourselves when we're ill - dragging ourselves into the office in a blaze of snotty glory, nearly passing out over a hot stove in order to feed the family. This is craziness. The world will not end if you don't go into work (and infect your colleagues!). The world will not end if your family eat take-out, ready meals or sandwiches for dinner. When you are ill you need to take care of yourself first and foremost and there is nothing wrong with that at all. So use your illness as an opportunity to practise self-love - and see how loving this makes you towards others as well.

Tips for self love: Treat yourself to glossy magazines and page-turning books. Eat and drink healthily. Take long baths. Take stock of all your achievements and reasons to feel grateful and proud.

And, to sum it all up . . .

All of the opportunities here are things we can and should do, whatever the state of our health. But the fact is, life is crazy-busy and chock-full of distractions. Illness gives us a break from the madness, a chance to cocoon ourselves away for a while. Instead of fighting it, embrace it for the chance it brings to boost your emotional health.

Dare to Daydream

I believe that daydreaming should be made a compulsory part of everyday life. Just as we eat our meals, clean our teeth and wash every day, so I think we should make regular time to daydream. Because our daydreams are where we plant the seeds for our future happiness.

Many years ago, I was a student at Liverpool University. Coming from London, this meant regular two and a half hour train journeys at the beginning and end of each term and at least once in between. I loved those journeys because I had some of my very best daydreams on them. It really was a case of '*All aboard the Daydream Express!*' as I'd find myself a seat by a window, put on my Sony Walkman (I told you it was a long time ago...) and immerse myself in my own dream bubble - only emerging for the occasional cup of tea from the buffet car. This week, I had to return to Liverpool for work. And as the train set off along that familiar track, I once again slipped into a marathon daydream. And as I did, I was struck by a truly beautiful realisation. The daydreams I'd had back on that same journey all those years ago had gone on to create the life I'm living today. They had planted the seeds for my present-day happiness.

Back on my student journeys, I'd dreamt mainly of story and character ideas, and one day being able to earn a living as professional writer. There was also a point in the journey, about 30 minutes outside of London, which I referred to in my mind as 'The Ruins'. It was when the train sped through a country station and past the crumbling ruins of an ancient building. I never knew what the building was, or paid attention to the name of the town. I just knew that I loved the look of it and the sense of mystery about the place. *One day, I want to live in a place like that*, I would daydream to myself.

On Monday, I was travelling up to Liverpool to take part in an author event. As I thought back to my teenage daydreams, I had to pinch myself to make sure I wasn't still dreaming. And as the train zoomed past 'The Ruins' I felt a shiver of excitement.

That then unknown, mysterious place is now my home town. The ruins are an ancient castle. I go there sometimes to write.

So today, and every day, make sure you make time to daydream.

Switch off your phone.
Take yourself offline.
And immerse yourself in a dream bubble.

You never know what future happiness you might be sowing.

See How Far You've Come

In today's fast-paced society we are constantly pressured to be more, acquire more and achieve more.

And as a consequence, we can often experience feelings of overwhelm and under-achievement.

For those times when life feels too big and you feel too small, try this simple exercise to help you get back on top...

See how far you've come

If you *still* haven't got that promotion / launched that business / found that dream job, take a moment to take stock.

What *have* you achieved?

What work *are* you proud of?

If you still haven't found Mr or Ms Right, take a moment to remember all of the romantic lessons you have learnt.

All of the experiences that have set you on the path to true love - and steered you away from the path to true disappointment.

If you still haven't achieved that dream weight, take a moment to appreciate the fact that you are *alive*.

Take a moment to see how far you've come.

Write your findings down so that they really sink in.

Life is not a race.

And for those times when it feels as though it is, let the tortoise (of *The Hare and the Tortoise* fame) be your coach.

When I was little, somebody gave me a tortoise made out of seashells. I keep that tortoise on my desk now, as a constant reminder that we don't need to 'hare' through life.

That actually, slow can be good.

Slow gives you time to enjoy the journey.

Slow gives you time to appreciate the lessons.

Slow gives you the chance to see how far you've come.

Climb Your Dream Mountain

Sometimes achieving a dream can feel like climbing a mountain. As in, it's really frickin' hard! Recently, I gave a Dare to Dream talk at a college in Paris. I wanted to give the students a simple exercise to show them how they could achieve their dreams. And so I created the Dream Mountain.

I'm sharing the Dream Mountain with you here today, so that you can get clarity in your own dreams too.

First of all, take a sheet of A4 paper and draw the outline of a mountain, complete with a snow-capped peak and a couple of clouds either side of the top.
Inside the snow-capped peak, write your dream. For example:

- *Write a novel*

- *Start my own business*

- *Graduate from college*

- *Fall in love*

- *Marry Niall from One Direction* (this dream might actually belong to my niece)

This isn't about creating a great work of art - it's what's going in and around the mountain that counts.

And what's going in and around the mountain is anything and everything that will help you achieve your dream.

Let's start with your ***Action Steps***.

So, you have your big dream at the top of your mountain - your action steps are the things you can do to start climbing your way up to achieving it.

If you think your dream will take at least a year to achieve, ask yourself what you could do within the next six months to help make it happen.

Write this somewhere inside your mountain, close to the top.

Then ask yourself what you could do towards that goal in the next three months.

Add this half way up the inside of your mountain.

Next, ask yourself what you could do in the coming month.

Write this in the bottom quarter of the mountain.

Beneath this, write what you could do towards achieving your dream this week.

Now, what could you do today?

Write this at the very bottom of the mountain. This is your first step towards the top.

But as any good mountaineer knows, you can't get to the peak by taking steps alone.

You need additional help. You need...

Your Mountain Guides

These are the people who will always be there to support you and encourage you with your dreams.

The people who want you to succeed - and won't feel threatened or jealous if you do (beware of those energy-suckers!).

Write their names around the edge of your mountain now.

Then, to complete your Dream Mountain, you need to fill in the clouds at the top with your *Inner Voice of Dreams*.

There's a good chance that when it comes to your dreams, your inner voice is far more likely to be one of doom - constantly telling you that you can't possibly achieve your goals and that you just don't have what it takes.

Once you've done so, write the positive statements inside your dream clouds. For example:

- *'I am a talented writer'*

- *I am a creative and successful entrepreneur'*

- *'I am intelligent and gifted'*

- *'I am infinitely loving and loveable'*

- *'I am exactly what Niall from One Direction is looking for in a wife!'*

Once you've finished, stick your Dream Mountain on your wall, or keep it somewhere you'll see it regularly.

Every time you feel that your dream has become insurmountable and your focus is starting to drift, look at your mountain and get re-inspired.

You *have* got what it takes to achieve your dream.

You *are* supported.

You just need to take it *one step at a time*.

The Power in Pursuing Your Passions

"Ask what makes you come alive and do that. Because what the world needs is people who have come alive."
Howard Thurman

My son is in the process of applying to universities.

In the UK, this involves choosing five universities, sending them your predicted grades and a personal statement and hoping that you'll receive some offers back.

My son just received his fifth offer. Five out of five, with no requests for an interview and one of the universities concerned lowering their usual grade requirements if he will accept their offer.

I'm not telling you this because I want to indulge in a proud mum moment, although I am - *very* proud.

I'm telling you because there's an important lesson at the heart of his success.

My son is not a 'straight A student'.

Not at all.

But what he does have is an absolute passion for the subject he wants to study.

And that passion shone through every single word in his personal statement. Even the commas looked jazzed.

When we do the things we're passionate about we shine.

But all too often, our passions become clouded by our fears.

I dropped out of uni and (temporarily) gave up on my passion for writing because I was afraid I wasn't good enough.

Now that I'm back on track with my writing dream I love helping others pursue their passions.

Because when we follow our passions, we do our best work, and we become our best selves, and we bring light and love to the world.

So, ask yourself right now, '*What makes me come alive?*'

Then ask yourself how you can build more of it into your life.

If you're a creative, write, play or paint it.

If you're an entrepreneur, develop and expand it.

And if you're a student ... study it.

Don't get lost in the dark clouds of '*I'm not good enough*' fears.

Think instead of how you're going to light up the world.

The Secret to a Wonderful Winter

I used to hate winter.

As soon as the remnants of Christmas were all bagged up and waiting for the bin men I would fall into a slump, only regaining my mojo sometime in March.

But not this year.

This year, I seem to have cracked the secret to having a really happy winter.

In a nutshell, it is this:

DON'T FIGHT IT!

Or, slightly more poetically:

Embrace it, with love.

True, winter isn't sassy like summer, golden like autumn or newborn like spring.

On the surface, winter can seem like a really stark place.

But only on the surface.

Dig a little deeper, and winter is full of riches.

Winter = stillness

And stillness = good (just ask any Buddhist, or yogi, or Zen Master)

Winter is the perfect time to practise mindfulness, by accepting it for what it is - *and* what it isn't.

It isn't going to be warm.

It isn't going to be germ-free.

For long periods of the day, it isn't going to be light.

Accept it - don't fight it.

And embrace the opportunities it brings.

Eat healthily and heartily: Make soups and stews crammed with seasonal veggies and herbs and feel your energy levels soar.

Get cosy: When it's cold and stormy outside, create an oasis of cosiness inside. Wear snug, woolly jumpers. Fill your home with flickering candles and fairylights. Invite friends round for impromptu dinners or parties. Re-read favourite books. Re-watch favourite films. Turn your living room into a disco and dance some fire into your belly. Turn your bedroom into a *boudoir* and _____ [*you fill in the blank!*]

Exercise gently: Take walks. Fill your lungs with cool, fresh air. Enjoy the pale sunshine and don't fight the rain.

Take stock: Write a list of all the things you are proud of. Bask in the glow of achievement.

Be still: Sit. Lie. Listen to your inner voice of wisdom. Get clear on your life and your dreams.

If you get ill, let yourself be ill: Don't be a Martha Martyr and drag yourself into work. Let your body do what it needs to do to fight the bug. And don't moan about it! Embrace the opportunity to mainline daytime TV and magazines. Embrace the opportunity to rest.

This winter, go with the flow … and let the flow be slow.

End the Year on a High by Counting Your Blessings and Learning Your Lessons

Somehow - don't ask me how - we are almost into December already.

But before your world becomes a crazy whirl of xmas shopping, Baileys-supping, turkey stuffing, party going, and mistletoe smooching, take a moment - a quiet moment - for you.

The end of November is the perfect time to pause and take stock of the fading year.

The perfect time to count your blessings, learn your lessons and figure out what and who you'd definitely like to keep in the new year - and what and who you'd like to let go of with love.

To make things super-simple for you, I've created a template below.

All you have to do is fill in the gaps.

Take some time when you know you won't be interrupted, copy the template into a notebook, or on to your pc, and let the words flow.

The best thing about this year has been....................

This year, I'm really proud of the way I....................

The most important lesson I've learnt is that....................

My greatest achievements have been....................

I'm really grateful to have had the love and support of....................

One way of behaving that hasn't served me this year has been....................

Next year, I shall replace this behaviour with....................

This year, a situation that hasn't brought out the best in me is....................

Next year, I shall change this for the better by....................

I'm disappointed by the way my relationship with....................has been this year.

Next year, I shall resolve this by....................

If I had to pick one positive word to sum this year up it would be....................

This year, I shall bring more love and joy to the world by....................

And if I had to pick one inspirational word / statement / quote to have as my motto for this year it would be....................

Here's to ending the year with a heart full of hope and gratitude, blissfully baggage-free.

This New Year, Step Away from the Resolutions

Hey, you! Yes, you! The one with the list of New Year's Resolutions longer than your arm. Stop what you're doing. Stop it right now!

I think I may well be the only life coach in existence to hate New Year's Resolutions.

Here's why...

It's the beginning of January, officially the grimmest month in the calendar - made all the grimmer by the fact that it comes straight after the party month of the year (a bit like watching an episode of *EastEnders* right after a Ben Stiller movie).

In the Northern hemisphere, it's one of the coldest, greyest months of the year. Even the most beautiful of landscapes can look ugly in January.

And what do we do to help brighten this starkest of months?

We resolve to half starve ourselves on detox diets.

We push our Christmas-bloated bodies to the limit in bootcamp-style fitness regimes.

Some people even give up chocolate - the horror!!

We set lists of goals so long we can't possibly hope to achieve them.

But today I'd like to suggest a gentler, more loving approach to the new year.

I think we should follow nature's example.

In January, you don't see plants trying to burst through the frozen soil in a desperate bid to start the year as they mean to go on.

In January, plants do the sensible thing. They stay protected from the harsh elements and bide their time.

Now, I'm not suggesting that we all bury ourselves in the garden until February comes, attractive as that might sometimes seem.

But what I am suggesting is that we use this month to stay nourished and take stock.

Eat well and heartily - don't starve.

Brighten the dark days with treats like chocolate. Yes, really.

Exercise gently. Practise yoga. Take walks. Swim. Dance. Don't batter your immune system with 'regimes'.

And instead of setting a mammoth list of goals that will leave you feeling overwhelmed and inadequate when you aren't able to achieve them, use this month to dream.

Shut out the cold and the rain and snuggle up with your dreams.

Play soft music and dance with your dreams.

Close your eyes and lie down with your dreams.

Create a post-it note dream board and play with your dreams.

Add random words . . . images . . . places . . . people.

Move them around.

Add new dreams into the mix.

Get messy.

Imagine freely.

Make your dreams for the new year flexible, creative and fun.

And read Danielle LaPorte's wonderful book, *The Desire Map*, to help shift your focus from what you want to achieve to *how you want to feel* this year.

Then, in February, when the world gets lighter and brighter and the sap starts rising, you can choose which dreams you'd like to manifest.

Start the new year softly and with a sense of fun.

Start as you mean to go on.

Free Yourself by Freeing Your Mind

At the beginning of January I was trying to get focused on what I wanted for the new year and, in a bid to keep it simple, I decided to try and hone it down to just one word.

The word that came to me, cutting like a bullet through the fug of *goals* and *to do lists* and *new year's effing resolutions*, was freedom.

FREEDOM.

For much of last year I'd laboured under a feeling of being trapped, but why?

The more I examined why I'd been feeling trapped, the more I realised it was all in my mind.

I was feeling trapped because of the thoughts I was having.

This was a revelation.

If I could change my thoughts then surely I could change how I was feeling.

I just had to make freedom my mantra.

I stuck the word **FREEDOM** on my bedroom wall, so I'd see it the moment I woke up.

I pasted it inside the cover of my journal.

I typed it into my screensaver.

FREEDOM, FREEDOM everywhere, urging me to change my thoughts and, consequently, my actions.

Every night before I went to sleep, I asked myself what I needed to do the next day in order to feel free.

Go to a dance class
Take myself off on a hike
Do something different
See someone different

Sometimes it was as simple as, *take yourself out for your coffee break instead of staying at home.*

And pretty soon I didn't have to pre-plan it; freedom became my default setting.

I'd instinctively try something new, deviate from the plan, break the rule, write from the heart.

And when I did find myself feeling trapped and frustrated with a situation, I trained myself to reboot my brain. Asking the question:

How can I think more freeing thoughts?

An example...

In January I launched a new project.

Normally when I launch something, I get a chronic case of the *'what if'*s.

What if nobody likes it / views it / buys it / shares it.

And instantly, I'm trapped in fear.

But this time, at the first sign of a *what if*, I'd replace the thought with something expansive and freeing, like '*build it and they shall come*' or '*what else can I do to make it helpful and fun?*'

Or I'd stop what I was doing and dance for half an hour.

And so my year has started full of sweetness and grace.

Instead of plodding or hamster-wheeling or racing through life, I feel as if I'm drifting - in the nicest possible way.

It's as if my thought-bubbles of freedom are carrying me along like hot air balloons.

All I have to do is relax and enjoy the ride.

Over to you...

What thoughts keep you trapped?

How can you change them to something more expansive?

Every night before you go to bed, ask yourself what one thing you could do tomorrow to make you feel free.

Do it.

Dear Dare to Dream: When Will Life Give Me a Break?

Dear Dare to Dream,

I keep daring to dream that life will just give me a break. I love life, I just want the chance to live it, nothing earth shattering, to be at peace and free from pain.

In the last 5 years I've dealt with cancer, and subsequent health problems and divorce (and its impacts on my kids). I'm not bitter, don't think the world is against me, things happen for a reason and you learn from them and use them as a positive.

But I'm getting tired of battling on and its taking its toll. Dealing with another health scare and I'm in a serious amount of pain, can't sleep. I'm so scared at yet another mountain to climb. There is so much I want to do and I know that whatever I'm faced with I will conquer but I'm so tired and I'm struggling more and more to keep going.

All I want to do is pack up and go back home to the sea, to be in a place where there isn't constant noise, where there's space to breathe, where I feel safe. But I can't move my children away from their dad, they've been through so much and no matter what I think about him I can't live with myself that I'd knowingly separate a dad from his children. My dad was never bothered about me and I ceased contact many years ago, sometimes you have to quit and let go. I know I need to keep going, but at the moment it's hard...

Life Lover

Dear Life Lover,

Reading your email reminded me of a saying my Christian friends often use:

'God never gives you more than you're able to handle.'

I don't really like this saying.

I don't really like this saying because sometimes *God / the Universe / Murphy's Law / Whatever You Believe In* gives us so effing much that we aren't able to handle it at all.

And you, Life Lover, have been given so much to handle lately, so many mountains to climb, I'm not surprised you're saying 'enough already'.

Two things shine out of your email at me:

your strength

and your love.

You've dealt with cancer and divorce and yet you aren't bitter.

You want to move on, you don't want to separate your children from their father; you put their needs before your own.

You are a wonderful human being.

But you're tired and scared and in pain.

You need a break; the space and peace and safety of the sea.

But you can't get there.

The good news is, you can make it come to you.

And here's how...

Several years ago, my partner was diagnosed with a brain tumour.

He had to have emergency surgery to remove the tumour and I can honestly say that day was the scariest of my life.

Watching him being taken down to theatre, not knowing if he'd make it through the operation, made me practically catatonic with fear.

As I waited on my own, my fear grew and grew. I didn't want to leave the hospital but I needed to do something to calm my anxiety.

So I took myself around the corner to Great Ormond Street Hospital.

My sister had spent a lot of time there with my niece and I remembered her telling me that the chapel was incredibly peaceful.

I wasn't a religious person but I was a desperate person so when I got to the chapel, I sat down, closed my eyes and asked for help - quietly, in my head.

'Please ... please help me to deal with this. Please help me to be strong for Steve.'

And that's when the miracle happened.

There were no heavenly choruses or lightning bolts. But I did experience the most incredible sensation of peace. Instantly.

It was like switching channels on a TV - one second I was fraught, exhausted and anxious, the next, I felt total and utter calm and the certain knowledge that everything was going to be okay.

I'm not sure how long I sat there for in the end but when I did finally leave, the peaceful feeling came with me.

Like a protective aura, it accompanied me back around the corner to Steve's hospital, up into the Intensive Care Unit and over to his bed - where I found him off his head on morphine singing football songs!

The operation had been a success but the diagnosis was as bleak as it comes: Melanoma. Terminal. Two months.

Although I have no idea what it is like to receive a cancer diagnosis as you have done, Life Lover, I do know what it is like to live with the fear of death hanging over a loved one.

I know all about waking up in the dead of night, panic gripping your chest like a vice. I know all about the anger and the depression and the sorrow.

But I also know that when you sit in stillness and go inside and ask for help, you receive it. No matter how crappy life gets.

So, although you might not be able to move back to the peace and space and quiet of the sea, you can find those things inside of you - any time.

My advice to you is this...

First, acknowledge how magnificent you are.

You've dealt with so much and yet you're still loving and living and daring to dream.

You're also clearly a wonderful mother and through your unselfishness, your children will benefit from two loving and involved parents despite your divorce.

You've faced cancer and come out fighting.

Take some time to truly acknowledge these achievements.

Buy yourself a gift - a piece of jewellery, perhaps - as a token of your pride. Every time you look at it be reminded of how incredible you are and all you deserve.

And secondly, find your own personal inner retreat through any or all of the following:

Prayer
Meditation
Walking
Free-writing
Nature
Dance (5 Rhythms and Biodanza are both great ways of dancing into a place of safety and love)
Yoga
Massage
Reiki
A soothing 'sea sounds' CD

When I was little, my mum held a shell to my ear so that I could hear the sound of the ocean inside it.

Of course, it wasn't really the sea.

According to Wikipedia, it was '*the noise of the surrounding environment, resonating within the cavity of the shell',* but to my five-year-old self it was utterly magical.

I truly believed that they were waves I was hearing. It didn't matter that it wasn't.

Finding the peace and safety of the sea inside of yourself is like creating your own personal super-power.

Whenever you're given more than you can handle, you instantly know what to do.

Go within.

Ask for help.

Seek the peace.

Over the years I've realised that, as long as we remember to ask for help, being given more than we can handle can be a blessing in (a very heavy!) disguise.

Because it teaches us that true strength and happiness and peace always come from within.

Because it stretches us into wiser, kinder, more loving human beings.

Just like you.

With love and prayers for a healthy and happy future,

Siobhan x

Part Two: Love

'Love has no other desire but to fulfil itself. But if you love and must needs have desires, let these be your desires: to melt and be like a running brook that sings its melody to the night. To know the pain of too much tenderness. To be wounded by your own understanding of love; and to bleed willingly and joyfully. To wake at dawn with a winged heart and give thanks for another day of loving.'

Kahlil Gibran

Love is an Inside Job

"You have to grow from the inside out. None can teach you, none can make you spiritual. There is no other teacher but your own soul."
Swami Vivekananda

I can remember exactly where I was, the moment I gave up looking for all of my happiness inside another person. I was hiding inside a pub toilet.

I was hiding inside a pub toilet from The Internet Date from Hell.

I won't bore you with the details but these are the *'What Not to Do'* tips I gleaned from that date:

- *Don't start talking about how much you hate your mother, ten minutes into a first date.*
- *Actually, don't start talking about how much you hate your mother* any *minutes into any date!*
- *Don't repeatedly refer to yourself in the third person.*
- *Don't stare pointedly at your date's chest for the duration*
- *Don't repeatedly rub your crotch – it implies inappropriate arousal or nasty infection. Either way, it's not good*

Anyway, so there I was, sat on the lid of the pub toilet, head in hands, thinking, *what am I doing here?* over and over.

The answer to that question was that I was looking for true-love-and-therefore-true-happiness there.

And, like most of the rest of the population, I believed that the only way I could get true-love-and-therefore-true-happiness was from another person.

One of the most common misconceptions we have about love is that it's some kind of possession we can only acquire from someone else.

If only I could find true love - then I'd feel complete, we say, frantically swiping our way through Tinder or winking our way through e-Harmony.

If only he / she loved me exactly the way I want them to, then I'd be happy, we say of our partners, instantly placing unreasonable and/or unachievable expectations upon them.

Not only is this notion wrong, but it can also be very perilous. Investing all of our happiness in the feelings and actions of another is a bit like leaving it at the edge of a blustery clifftop and hoping it won't get swept away.

We have no control over other people - we may sometimes wish that we did but we don't. So, if we've invested all of our happiness in someone loving us and then they decide that they don't - or they turn out to be very different to our expectations - the result can be devastating.

I felt so depressed that night in the pub toilet because I'd invested so much hope in the date. Instead of viewing it as a potentially fun night out with another human being, I'd filled my head with dreams that I might be about to meet 'Mr Right'. When he turned out to be Mr I-Hate-My-Mum-and-Speak-About-Myself-in-the-Third-Person-and-Possibly-Have-a-Genital-Infection, I felt crushed with disappointment.

And as well as leaving you wide open to disappointment, this way of living and loving sets you up for a lifetime of need.

I need to meet my other half.
I need them to be perfect.
I need them to love me.

I need.
I need.
I need.

As I hid in the pub toilet that night, I had the certain realisation that I'd been looking for love in all the wrong places. And I was so fed-up with the constant disappointment I was determined to find out where the right place was.

After a lengthy search, that led me to meditation pillows and church pews and dance classes and drumming circles and yoga mats and even Hemel Hempstead, this is what I found...
Love is an energy that exists within all of us and we're free to bask in it at any time, single or no.

You can't be truly happy until you fully claim this love for your own and truly love yourself.

By seeking love from another in order to experience love for ourselves we've got it all the wrong way round.

Exercise: Feeling the Love Inside

Take some time when you know you won't be interrupted and sit in stillness with your eyes closed. Take a few deep breaths, in through the nose and out through the mouth, then think of someone you truly love with no complications. Picture them sitting or standing in front of you and notice any changes in your body as you do so.

Do you start feeling more relaxed?
Do they bring a smile to your face?

Now focus on your heart area. Feel it opening and expanding as you think of this person with love. Feel the warmth of your love radiating throughout your body like the rays of the sun.

Really bask in its glow as you turn the love you are feeling on to yourself. Visualise love entering every cell of your body, from the tips of your toes to the top of your scalp. See yourself filling up with love's golden light. Keep breathing slowly, in through the nose and out through the mouth, enjoying the warmth and relaxation that resting in love can bring.

When you're ready, open your eyes.

Know that you can do this exercise whenever life leaves you feeling battered and bruised and in need of a hug
.

Know that you can do this exercise whenever you're in need of love.

When in Doubt, Ask: What Would LOVE Do?

'Wherever you are, and whatever you do, be in love.'
Rumi

If I had to pick one question that has helped me the most in life (apart from *'Do you have chocolate?'*) it is *'What would love do?'* Any time I feel like I'm about to blow a gasket or be overcome with fear or swept away on a tide of sorrow, I ask *'What would love do?'* and I instantly feel better.

When I'm about to give a talk to hundreds of people and I'm overwhelmed by the enormity of the occasion, *'What would love do?'* reminds me to place my focus solely on the audience and how I can help them, rather than stressing about whether I'll forget what to say or fall over on stage.

When an ex antagonises me and my head starts filling with thoughts of recrimination and blame, *'What would love do?'* reminds me that we're all human - even exes (*who knew?!)* - and if I act with compassion the situation is instantly defused.

When I'm confronted with a surly shop-assistant who seems to have been taught that the customer is always wrong, *'What would love do?'* reminds me that there's probably a great deal of pain behind their scowl and helps me smile sweetly in the face of their hostility.

When I have an important decision to make work-wise and I'm terrified of making the wrong choice, *'What would love do?'* gets me to tune into my heart, the best career coach in the business, and I make the choice guaranteed to bring the most joy.

When I feel stretched to the limit and about to crack, *'What would love do?'* makes me turn off my phone, run myself a bath and do absolutely nothing for hours on end.

Try it for yourself and see.

Take a situation or dilemma that's currently playing on your mind and ask, *'What would love do?'*

Listen carefully for the answer ... then do it.

Remove Your Barriers to Love

"Your task is not to seek for Love, but merely to seek and find all the barriers within yourself that you have built against it."
Rumi

When I was little, my parents would read me stories. Stories about glass slippers, and chocolate factories, and imaginary worlds through the back of a wardrobe.

But although I didn't realise it at the time, these weren't the only stories I was being told.

In witnessing our parents' actions, we create other stories in our minds. Stories about life and stories about love and stories about how loveable we are. Sometimes these can be wonderful stories, ending in happily ever afters. If our parents are able to express love freely, we absorb the story that we are entirely loveable and we're able to grow up expecting nothing less.

But if our parents find it hard to show love; if they've been traumatised by pain and loss, if they've covered their heart in armour-plating, or if they numb their pain with alcohol or drugs, then it's all too easy to absorb the fairy-tale that we're not loveable.

And these fear-based fairy-tales can be grimmer than Grimm's. Often, we carry them with us our entire lives; time and time again selling ourselves short when it comes to love and life because our impressionable and immature minds took it for granted that they had to be true.

Once upon a time, a father was unable to hug his daughter or ever tell her that he loved her.

Moral of the story: *The child just wasn't loveable enough and she deserved to live unhappily ever after.*

It's not just our parents who cause us to create these fear-based fairy-tales. It can be other family members, or teachers or even friends.

Once upon a time, a teacher repeatedly mocked a child in front of his entire class. 'Your story is rubbish.' 'This homework is no good.' 'Look at the state of you,' the teacher said, over and over again.

Moral of the story: *The child just wasn't loveable enough and he deserved to live unhappily ever after.*

But by choosing to believe these fear-based fairy-tales, we forget the most important and truest story about ourselves. And that is:

Once upon a time, you were born with the incredible capacity to love and be loved.
Moral of the story: *You are entirely loveable and you deserve to live happily ever after.*

When I was a child, my father never told me that he loved me. Not ever. I now know that this wasn't because he didn't. It was because he couldn't. He came from a generation of men who were taught to hold back emotionally. But I didn't understand this when I was young. And so I absorbed the fear fairy-tale that he didn't tell me he loved me because he didn't love me. And I formed the conclusion that this was because I was unloveable.

When a fear fairy-tale becomes a collected works
Once we've established the fear fairy-tale that we aren't loveable there's a real danger that we start compiling a collection of other related stories around it. *'I'm Not Loveable: The Collected Works'* if you like. Allow me to share with you another fairy-tale from my own personal collection, a tragic tale entitled: *The Slow Dance of Sorrow*.

When I was about twelve, a school friend called Jackie had a birthday disco. (It was the eighties. Along with furry dice and Rubik's cubes, birthday discos were all the rage.) All of my school friends were at the disco and it was a really fun night - until the slow dancing began.

One by one, my friends began pairing up with boys and shuffling around awkwardly to the dulcet tones of Michael Jackson singing *One Day in Your Life* (I was so traumatised, that song still makes me feel sick every time I hear it). Two by two, they all paired up, until there was just one person left standing on her own. Me. It was the longest, most embarrassing three hours of my life - at least, it felt like three hours. And as I stood pressed against the wall, trying to be swallowed up by the darkness, I started composing another fear fairy-tale.

None of the boys want to dance with you because you're not as pretty as the other girls. They don't want to dance with you because you're ugly. They don't want to dance with you because you're not dance-with-able. And you're not dance-with-able because you're not loveable.

If our self-esteem is already fragile it doesn't take much to make us add to our collection of fear fairy-tales. A more confident person would have laughed it off, reasoning that there was an odd number of people at the disco so someone had to be left out, but not me. I instantly leapt to the conclusion that there was something wrong with me.

And throughout my teenage years, I continued adding fear fairy-tales to my collection, like a very morbid version of Mills & Boon.

The Girl Whose Father Didn't Love Her
The Girl Whose Mother Left
The Slow Dance of Sorrow
Fourteen and Never French-kissed!

Often, we don't even realise we're doing it. The stories we tell ourselves just become part of our inner narrative. But before we're able to properly love ourselves, we have to get clear on the ways in which we've been blocking this love by telling ourselves lies.

When I look back on my own fear fairy-tales now, I'm able to see that every one of them is a work of fiction. My dad did love me, he just didn't know how to verbalise it. The fact that no boys asked me to dance at a disco in someone's living room when I was twelve-years-old does not mean that I'm a hideous unloveable troll who should slink off to live under a bridge. Getting to the truth of the stories we tell ourselves when it comes to love is massively liberating and a fundamental first step in being able to love ourselves and others fearlessly.

Re-Write Your Love Stories

What fear-based fairy-tales are you still clinging on to from your past?

In which ways do you believe yourself to be unloveable?

Take a moment to jot down any negative beliefs you hold about yourself, such as:

I'm not good enough.
I'm not attractive enough.
I'm not clever enough.
I'm not interesting enough.

Now dig down to discover the stories behind these beliefs.

Who (intentionally or unintentionally) first caused you to question your loveability in these ways?
Was it a parent or other family member, a teacher or friend?
Now dig a little deeper to get to the real truth.

When we're younger, our impressionable brains soak up stories like sponges. We unquestioningly believe in Father Christmas and the Tooth Fairy and pumpkins that turn into golden coaches. We also unquestioningly believe our fear-based fairy-tales about love. It's time for you to explode the myths you've been telling yourself. And the best way to do this is to ask yourself the simple question:

Can I absolutely know this to be true?

If your father was never able to tell you that he loved you, is this really proof that you are unloveable? Or does it actually say more about him?

If your teacher ridiculed you, is this really proof that you are unloveable? Or does it actually say way more about their state of mind?

If a friend constantly undermined you, is this really proof that you are unloveable? Or does their need to do this actually say way more about their own insecurities?

Once you've realised that your fear fairy-tales are exactly that - fairy-tales - you're free to start believing in your true love story. That you are infinitely loving and loveable. Start writing it down now:

I am infinitely loveable because...

I Am Love Meditation

As we've established, the biggest misconception there is when it comes to love is that it's some kind of external product that you're only able to acquire from other people.

The truth is, you are always able to access love in your life because it exists within you.

It exists within all of us.

Life makes it very easy to forget this though. Here are just some of the ways in which it likes to throw a spanner in the works:

The boss who undermines you. The partner who criticises you. The unexpected, overdraft-busting bill. The scary diagnosis. Loneliness. Being misunderstood. Being judged. The redundancy. The break-up.

All of these and many, many more can leave you up to your neck in fear and completely cut adrift from love. And when you feel cut adrift from love it's all too easy to sink deeper and deeper into fearful thoughts about yourself and your life.

One of the best ways I've found to speedily find my way back to a state of love is through meditation. But I'm very aware that for a lot of people, the word 'meditation' only causes them more stress. Visions of blissed out yogis sitting painlessly in the lotus position for hours on end, achieving inner enlightenment as effortlessly as popping out for a sandwich, can be extremely intimidating, especially if the minute you attempt to meditate and achieve inner calm, your mind starts going bonkers.

The first thing I'd like to say about this is, don't panic. Everyone encounters this kind of mental chatter when they meditate, especially at first.

The first time I attempted to do a guided meditation it went something like this:

Meditation: Take a deep breath.
Me: *I bet this doesn't work.*
Meditation: Feel your body relax.
Me: *My knee is really aching.*
Meditation: Let go of any tension.
Me: *Now my shoulder's aching too. I wonder if I'm getting arthritis? How old do you have to be to get arthritis? What should I make for dinner tonight...? What's good for arthritis...?*
Meditation: Picture golden light flooding into your body through the top of your head.
Me: *Oily fish... I bet that's good for arthritis...*
Meditation: Feel that light filling your body.
Me: *I'm not sure about the music they're using for this meditation, it sounds a bit like the soundtrack to a sci-fi movie ... I wonder if there is any alien life form out there?*
Meditation: Empty your mind of all thoughts.
Me: *What? How? Surely the only time you empty your mind of all thoughts is when you're dead. Or asleep. No, when you sleep you still have dreams. How can I empty my mind of all thoughts? That doesn't make sense!*
Meditation: Just relax.
Me: *How?!*
Meditation: Picture anyone who has been causing you stress, floating away from you down a river.
Me: *Okay, I can do that.*
Meditation: Picture them drifting further and further away.
Me: *What if they can't swim? What if they start to drown?*
Meditation: Let go of all situations that are causing you stress. Visualise them floating away from you down the river too.
Me: (*visualising my faulty car, my damp-riddled house and the entire Inland Revenue floating down a river*) *I need to go to the toilet.*
Meditation: Picture the water flowing past you, carrying it all away.

Me: *Enough with the water imagery – I'm going to frickin' wet myself!*

You get the picture. So if you've struggled with meditation in the past, you most definitely aren't alone.

The key is to *not* attempt to empty your mind of all thoughts - that way sheer madness lies. Instead, keep allowing your thoughts to come but concentrate on disengaging from them and simply observing them come and go. This way, you're able to let your thoughts drift through your mind without getting bogged down in them. If thoughts of what to cook for dinner or how much you hate your next door neighbour pop up, don't resist them, don't feel guilty for thinking when you should be meditating, just watch them, the same way you would watch a cloud skim across the sky, with the detachment of a disinterested observer:

Oh, there goes that thought about how much I hate my neighbour. And here comes the one about the tax bill...

Sitting in stillness and letting your thoughts drift by in this way helps you get to a much more relaxed and receptive state. And this can be transformative when it comes to reconnecting with the love inside of you.

Exercise: 'I Am Love' Meditation

Using the mantra, *'I am Love'* in a meditation is a great way of building your self-love and tapping into a more loving state. So, starting with the premise that it is perfectly okay for negative thoughts to come up and totally impossible to completely empty your mind, find a comfortable and peaceful place to sit up straight, or if you prefer, lie down. Close your eyes and place one hand on your stomach. Take a deep breath, in through the nose. You should feel your stomach expand on the inhale. Then exhale through the mouth and feel your stomach sink.

Repeat this slow, deep breathing, in through the nose and out through the mouth, until you've got into a regular and calming rhythm.

Remove your hand from your stomach and turn your palms upwards. Continue to breathe slowly and deeply, in through the nose and out through the mouth. Observe any negative thoughts you may be having. Picture them in a cartoon-style thought-bubble above your head. Now picture them drifting off. Keep repeating this exercise for every thought that pops up.

Simply observe it and let it go.

Let your deep breathing help you with this, keeping you focused and relaxed. In through the nose and out through the mouth. Then start repeating the mantra '*I am Love*' on every in-breath and every out-breath.

Inhale: *I am Love*
Exhale: *I am Love*
Inhale: *I am Love*
Exhale: *I am Love*

Any time a thought pops up, picture it drifting away from your head like a cloud and return to the mantra:

I am Love
I am Love
I am Love

Do this for at least five minutes.
Do this until you truly start to believe it.

You ARE Love.

Forgiveness - the Fast Lane to Self-Love

'You can't build joy on a feeling of self-loathing.'
Ram Dass

There are various 'superpowers' we have at our disposal when it comes to accessing love. One of the biggest of these is forgiveness. And when it comes to self-love, forgiveness can provide speedy and permanent breakthroughs.

When we forgive ourselves, we accept that we have full responsibility for our lives and our actions and we release ourselves from pain, guilt and regret. Forgiveness sets us free from self-loathing, enabling us to move into a place of self-loving.

The first step in self-forgiveness is acknowledging where you have done wrong. I'm going to use an example from my own life here to demonstrate.

When I was in my early twenties, I cheated on my boyfriend. I wish I could make some kind of justification here, like he'd treated me badly or he'd cheated on me too, but I can't. He was a kind and lovely person. I, on the other hand, was trapped in a downward spiral of anger and self-absorption. The more loving he was towards me, the more resentful I became of him. I've subsequently learnt that this is a recognised behaviour in people who believe themselves to be unloveable. If somebody shows them love they are completely unable to handle it. *If you can love someone as unloveable as me, then you must be a real loser*, so the f***ed up logic goes. I am deeply ashamed of how I treated my boyfriend in the last couple of months of our relationship. I acted like a spoilt brat. And I finally left him for another man. But, as I said, there was a slight overlap in the relationships. I cheated on him with the man I ended up leaving him for.

For many, many years, I was unable to forgive myself for what I'd done. When my subsequent partner, who I ended up marrying, went on to cheat on me, I remember thinking that this was karma in action. That I was getting no more than I deserved. I became trapped in a downward spiral of self-loathing. When it crossed my mind that I ought to forgive myself, I immediately dismissed it. How could I forgive myself for what I'd done? I now knew how awful it was to be cheated on. I now knew exactly what kind of pain I'd caused. What I'd done seemed even more unforgiveable. But by coming to this conclusion, I was making an all too common mistake.

Forgiveness does not mean condoning an action or behaviour. It means letting go of the resultant anger and pain, whilst continuing to acknowledge that the behaviour was wrong. And in this way, it is one of the most powerful acts of love we can ever perform.

For years, I'd hated myself for what I'd done. Now I asked myself, where was the opportunity to love and forgive myself instead? I looked back on the angry young woman I'd been then and I looked back on all the events that had led to me choosing to behave in that way and I felt so sad. But I also felt compassion.

What I did was wrong but *we are not our actions*. And recognising this fact is liberating because it means that we always have the opportunity to start over again.

We always have the opportunity to return to love.

And one thing I learnt when I looked back at what I had done with forgiveness, is that when we are filled with self-loathing it is impossible to properly love another. We therefore have an obligation to love and forgive ourselves so that we can fully love and forgive others.

Exercise: Forgive Yourself

Take a moment to identify something you need to forgive yourself for.

Understand that by forgiving yourself you are not condoning what you did, you're simply recognising that you are not your actions and you're freeing yourself from any associated guilt and pain.

The fact is, becoming eaten up with guilt and pain doesn't serve anyone. If anything, it just perpetuates your negative self-image and makes you all the more likely to act from a place of fear again.

Follow these simple steps to release yourself...

Step One: Acknowledge and Apologise

First of all, acknowledge what you've done wrong. If there's any way you can try to make things right and apologise for your actions, do so. If this is impossible because you're unable to contact the person or people concerned, then writing an apology letter to that person can have an equally cathartic effect - even if you aren't able to send it. Of course, it could be that you need forgiveness for the way you've treated *yourself*. If so, write an apology letter to you. Pour all of your sorrow and regret into the letter. Don't make any excuses, step up and take full responsibility for the way you've behaved. All too often, we keep guilt buried deep within us like a tumour. Acknowledging it and thereby removing it in this way, is extremely healthy.
It stops it from growing and taking us over. Don't let the past sabotage your future. Acknowledge what you've done to yourself or another by writing it down now.

Don't get sucked into yet more negative self-talk, just state the facts in simple black and white:

I cheated...
I lied...
I stole...
I hurt...
I let myself down by...

And then write, *I'm sorry*.

Step Two: Find the Love

How can you love yourself in spite of what you've done?
How can you find pity and compassion in your heart?
Write down everything you can think of. All of the factors that
led to you making that wrong decision or choice. These things
aren't excuses or justifications. They are explanations to help
you find the love and compassion needed to forgive. In my own
case, I thought of the things that had happened to me as a child
that caused me to create the fear fairy-tale that I wasn't
loveable. I thought of how angry and closed-off this had made
me become. And I was able to find compassion for that
frightened young woman.

Step Three: Forgive

Take a moment to close your eyes and visualise yourself doing
the thing that needs your forgiveness. Then visualise sending
love to yourself in that moment in time. This can be in whatever
way works for you - I like to visualise golden light pouring down
on myself. Then tell yourself over and over again (silently or out
loud): *I forgive you*. Keep on saying it until you truly mean it.
Relax into the lightness of being set free. Know that by doing
this, you aren't just freeing yourself from guilt and pain. You're
freeing yourself to be able to love and forgive others too.

Loving My Single Parent Self

For several years, I was a single working parent. And the 'working' part of my life included a nightmare commute into London on an airless train that smelt of canned body odour and bad breath.

One evening as I sat slumped on the packed train home, my flushed face pressed against the window, I realised that most of my fellow commuters were men. And most of them were wearing wedding rings.

I pictured the owners of their matching rings waiting for them at home, all smiley-faced and serene as they bathed the kids and prepared the dinner.

Then I pictured my son, home alone, eating dry cereal from the box - probably dropping dry cereal from the box all over the floor - waiting for me to come home and put on my mum hat.

As I sat there on that train, the thought of coming home and having to cook dinner, pack lunches, help with homework and clean up made me feel weary to my bones.

I looked at my bare ring finger and saw failure tattooed there in invisible ink.

Invisible to everyone apart from me.

I felt myself crumpling inside.

Then I took out my notepad and began to write.

I wrote a list of all the reasons I should love my single parent self. All the reasons I should feel proud.

The list went on for two pages.

The following day I bought myself a ring.

It has success written on it in invisible ink.

Invisible to everyone apart from me.

Loving Kindness - the Instant Happiness Hit

Let me tell you a secret...

Any time you feel fear pulling you down and dragging you under, you can get an instant hit of happiness by performing an act of loving kindness.

Try an experiment now.

Take out your phone and send someone a loving text.

Tell someone that you love them.

Tell someone how grateful you are for them.

Thank someone simply for being.

Then press send and see how it makes you feel.

Loving Men, Loving Women

Once upon a time, I went to a meeting in my local church.

The meeting was about how to live a Christian life. I wasn't a Christian but I was curious.

We were all given a questionnaire to help us see how near or far we were from achieving the ideal Christian life.

It was all going well until I came upon this question:

"Men, do you feel as if you are a good leader of your family?"

'What does this mean?' I asked the group. 'Why doesn't it say men *and* women?'

A middle-aged man sitting near me replied, 'Because in Christian families the man should be the leader.'

I instantly frowned. 'But why? Why can't men and women be equal within a family?'

'Because someone has to be the dominant one,' the man snapped back. 'That's the trouble with life today - there's far too many strong women about.'

He said the words 'strong women' the way you might say 'smelly turds'.

I was genuinely shell-shocked.

The thing that had made me curious about Christianity - the reason I was at the meeting to find out more - was the pure Love and simplicity I'd discovered at the heart of Jesus' teachings.

The venom in this man's voice and the fact that he - and the church - should see the need for women to be subservient within a marriage was hugely depressing.

But sure enough, it says in the Bible that, in marriage, a woman should 'submit to her husband'.

Several days later, I went out for lunch with a friend of mine, a young man in his twenties who was also at the church meeting. This man is one of the most loving and spiritual people I know. Surely he wouldn't agree with this ancient teaching?

'Actually, I do,' he told me quietly. 'As a man, I want to protect and provide for my family. I want to have that role. I want to feel needed.'

What he said really made me stop and pay attention. Here was someone I really liked and respected saying something I found almost impossible to comprehend - I knew I couldn't just dismiss it, I needed to give it some serious thought.

So I went home and thought and this is what I came up with:

Men and women are different.

But actually, our differences complement each other perfectly. As long as we fill our hearts with love and respect for each other.

And if we fill our hearts with love and respect for each other...

...there's no need for anyone to 'submit' to the other.

Women, love men.
Love them for their strength, love them for their drive. Love them for their clear thinking and their desire to provide. Love them for their vulnerability too.

Men, love women.
Love them for their strength, love them for their drive. Love them for their intuition and their emotion and their desire to nurture. Love them for their vulnerability too.

We are all people.

And - when we can get past all the bullshit prejudices and stereotypes - we are all Love.

(Later that day I asked my seventeen-year-old son if he felt that he'd need future romantic partners to submit to him. He looked at me like I was crazy. My heart filled with hope...)

Dating: To Text or Not to Text, that Should *Never* Be the Question

So, you've gone on a date with someone you really like and it went soft focus, rom com montage well.

As soon as you get home you want to text them and thank them for a great evening.

But before you can begin to type, fear starts tapping on your shoulder, whispering things like:

You can't tell them how you feel!
What if they don't feel the same?
What if they don't reply?
What if it makes you look desperate and uncool?

So you put your phone away and order a copy of *Women Who Love Too Much* from Amazon - next day delivery.

Meanwhile, your date has no idea how you're feeling.

But suppose you get fear to shut the hell up and you're able to come from a more loving place.

You send the text. You tell your date you had a great time.

Really, what is the worst that can happen?

They don't reply.

Well, then maybe they aren't who you thought they were after all.

They do reply but tell you that they find the fact that you texted so soon really uncool and desperate and therefore don't want to see you ever again.

Er, ditto!

They do reply, and tell you that they had a great time too.

Bingo!

Love isn't a game.

It's far too precious and special to be played with.

It deserves to be kept real.

You deserve it to be real.

And this requires honesty and courage and passion.

So the next time you've been on a date that's gone really well, send the text and feel proud for being a Love super hero.

Walk Into Love

Today, when I woke up, I felt fear tugging at my pillow.

'You have a book to finish in four weeks,' it hissed. *'Four weeks! You'll never do it. There's not enough time.'*

'Not enough time.'
'Not enough time.'

I felt my brain shrink with fear. This is not good when you're hoping to be creative. Creative brains need to expand until there is no horizon. I pulled myself out of bed, sat in front of my computer, and froze. Thankfully, due to my inactivity, my screensaver popped up in front of me.

WHAT WOULD LOVE DO? it very helpfully asked.

Hmm, love would do something fun like go for a walk along the canal and feed the ducks, I thought to myself.

So that's what I did.

And as soon as I saw the lush green leaves and the bright blue sky and the sun glimmering on the water...

As soon as I heard the chirp of the birds and the chug of the canal boats...

As soon as I smelt the freshly cut grass and the sun-baked earth...

As soon as I fed the fluffy yellow ducklings...

My mind began to unfurl.

And with every step I took, I felt closer to love and further from fear.

Closer to love and further from fear.

And I realised that actually, I'm part of something far, far bigger than my little brain could ever possibly comprehend.

And actually, in this grandest of grand scheme of things, deadlines and word counts are smaller than the smallest grain of pollen floating on the breeze.

Then I went home and wrote.

The Recipe for a Loving Life

Take one cup of gratitude.

Add a pinch of patient acceptance (or however many pinches are necessary. Sometimes, it may take a handful).

Stir in a generous helping of forgiveness.

Then add the mixture to a pot of humility (because it's not about you - it's all about Love).

Season with compassion.

Sprinkle Your Food with Love and Gratitude – an Introduction to Mindfulness

"If you truly get in touch with a piece of carrot, you get in touch with the soil, the rain, the sunshine. You get in touch with Mother Earth and eating in such a way, you feel in touch with true life, your roots and that is meditation. If we chew every morsel of our food in that way we become grateful and when you are grateful you are happy."
Thich Nhat Hanh

I don't think it would be an exaggeration to say that over the past few decades, the pace of life has shifted up several gears.

Now we're all hurtling along in the fast lane, multi-tasking, working longer hours than ever, whilst simultaneously reporting it all on our numerous social media accounts.

And this change in pace has been reflected in our eating habits, with supermarket shelves filling with 'fast foods', 'convenience foods' and 'ready meals'. We can even buy our veggies ready washed, peeled and chopped. I'm just waiting for Marks and Spencer to start offering a 'pre-digested' range.

But this hectic pace isn't just leaving us at the risk of indigestion, it's bad for our mental health too. Stress, anxiety and depression are all rapidly on the rise.

The fact is, us humans weren't built to cope with the manic pace of the internet age. We need regular time to be human's *be*ing, not endlessly doing.

Mindfulness is a wonderful tool that can help counter the stress of modern living; an ancient practice designed to bring your focus back to the present moment.

And a really enjoyable way to practice mindfulness is when you're eating.

Instead of shoveling your barely chewed food down your throat whilst sending that email, answering that call, Instagram-ing that soft-focus image of your meal and tweeting about how **#tasty** it is, place all of your attention on simply being there with your food.

Don't read anything, type anything, or say anything, just look at the food in front of you and think for a moment about everything that has happened to bring it to your plate.

Think of all the people who have made it possible.
The farmer. The baker. The shop-worker.
And give thanks to them.

Then take a bite of your food and really savour it.
Focus on the different textures and flavours and what they feel like on your tongue.

Feel gratitude for the experience.
Feel gratitude for the fact that you have food in a world where so many are starving.

As you slowly enjoy bite after bite, feel yourself relax.

Feel yourself fill with thanks.
For the food.
For the sustenance.
For the opportunity to just be, in the moment.

Love Life Fiercely in the Face of Illness

Today, I found out that my friend Michelle's leukemia has come back.

Five years ago, Michelle was diagnosed with leukemia for the first time. The way she dealt with that diagnosis was one of the most inspiring things I've ever witnessed.

Even when her body was ravaged by chemo, even when the doctors told her to go home and die, she refused to give in. 'I've had worse hangovers than that chemo,' she said defiantly from her hospital bed. 'Double what you've been giving me. I can take it.'

And she did.

She took it and she beat it and then she lived her life so fiercely and beautifully it tugged at my heart and brought tears to my eyes. After her bone marrow transplant, Michelle walked 100km from London to Brighton to raise money for a leukemia charity. She walked all night and half of the next day until her feet bled. She raised thousands of pounds. She went back to work and got promoted and started training for a job trading on the stock market - one of her life-long dreams. She rejoined her netball team and arranged more charity fund-raisers and bought a new property.

And now it's come back.

The leukemia that she thought she'd driven from her body has snuck back in when no-one was watching. And all I want to do is cry.

This evening, I walked home from the station along the canal. And with every beautiful sight I saw, I felt a stab of pain. What if Michelle doesn't make it out of hospital this time?

What if she never gets to see sunlight sparkling on water, or a waxy green leaf or a flower in bloom again?

Then I came across a family of swans – the mum and dad, white and majestic, their two chicks, ash grey balls of fluff.

And it reminded me that we are all constantly part of an endless cycle.

Birth and death.
Death and rebirth.

It started to rain.

But I left my umbrella in my bag.

Michelle might die.

But she might not.

And as the summer rain mingled with my tears, I realised something really important.

As long as there are baby swans and summer showers, as long as you keep on walking forwards, even with tears streaming down your face, as long as you love life fiercely and with everything you've got, then there is always hope.

Love Like a Dog

Two months ago, my beloved dog Max was put to sleep.

Since he's been gone I've spent a lot of time thinking about him and what he meant to me and the one over-riding realisation I've been left with is how much he taught me about love. And, more broadly speaking, how much dogs can teach *us* about love.

In today's society, love is all too often compartmentalised. There's the love that you have for your family members, there's spiritual love and of course, there's romantic love. And often, we are encouraged to love differently, according to which category the recipient of our love falls into. For instance, romantic love is frequently associated with need. You often hear people talking about their 'ideal partner' - and trotting out a well-rehearsed list of demands.

He must have a good sense of humour.
She must be blonde.
He has to earn at least £x per year.
She has to be into stamp-collecting etc, etc...

But, when you stop to think about this, it hardly seems like the ideal starting point for a romantic match. If you're already making demands before you've even met the person, you seem almost destined for disappointment if they fail to make the grade. By focusing on what other people can give to us when it comes to love, aren't we missing the point?

The thing that struck me most about a dog's love is how uncomplicated and unconditional it is.Whenever I'd get home, Max would rush to greet me, tail wagging furiously as he nuzzled my legs with his nose.If I was home a little later than normal he didn't sulk. He didn't stop his tail from wagging, in a *'this'll show her'* way.

Dogs don't know how to play mind games. They don't know how to withhold love - it just pours out of them unconditionally.

In the seven years I was lucky enough to have Max I went through some real highs and lows. But the one constant through all of that was the bond between us. Day after day, rain or shine, we would go for our walks together and I would often look at our shadows, cast long on the ground in front of us, and it would be such a reassuring sight. *We're still here, and we're still walking,* I'd think to myself. *We're still here, and we're still walking.*

One time on a walk together, a drunk guy started shouting at me. My good-natured, placid dog transformed before my eyes, snarling and snapping at him until he'd run away. Another time, when Max was a lot older and getting frail, two Alsations went for him as we walked past their house. This time, I was the one who was transformed, feeling the sudden protective urge of a lioness towards her cub, throwing myself into the fray and pulling them off him - something I never would have thought I was brave enough to do before.

But this is another thing I've learnt. When you are loved unconditionally and without demand, it becomes a beautiful cycle, as you are able to return that love in kind without a second thought. And now Max is no longer here. When I walk in the sun or moonlight I only see one shadow on the ground in front of me. But I still feel his presence all around me - still loving and protecting me. And the lessons he has taught me about love will continue to ripple out to everyone around me.

And hopefully now to you too...

In Times of Need, Pray to Love

I used to think that prayer was strictly the preserve of the religious, after all, how can you pray if you don't have a God to pray to? But then one day, when my partner was seriously ill, I got desperate. So I hit my knees and I prayed.

'Please don't let him die,' I begged. *'Please, please don't let him die.'*

Almost immediately, I was filled with a feeling of indescribable peace. It was the kind of experience I'd heard religious people talk about. But I wasn't religious.

Sometime later, I was facing a serious work dilemma. It was tying my brain in knots and none of my friends could help me find clarity. In the end, I prayed again. I wasn't exactly sure who I was praying to but again, I was desperate.

'Please help me make the right decision.' I asked. *'Please show me what to do.'*

The response wasn't as immediate this time. I got back up and set about my day. But a couple of hours later, the answer came to me. It was loving and wise and gave me instant clarity after weeks of doubt.

Now, whenever I'm in need, I hit my knees and pray. I pray for help. I pray for wisdom. I pray for clarity. I pray for strength. Sometimes I pray for a miracle, if that's what the situation requires, and then I take the time to listen (*because taking the time to listen for the answer is just as vital as asking the question*). Sometimes the answer comes quickly, sometimes it takes a few hours. But it always comes. I don't know where it's coming from. Maybe it's an inner wisdom. Maybe it's from something outside of me. All I know is that it works. Every time.

Try it for yourself and see.

If there's something currently bugging you; something causing you doubt or confusion or fear, get on to your knees and pray for guidance and help.

If you're not religious, think of it as praying to Love. Love with a capital L.

Then keep your eyes and ears wide open for the answer.

And know that it will come.

Falling Into a Human Safety Net of Love

"A friend is someone who knows all about you and still loves you."
Elbert Hubbard

Every so often, life will knock you sideways.

The unexpected loss of a job, or a relationship, or a loved one. A shocking diagnosis. A betrayal. A bitter bolt from the blue.

It's at times like these that fear can be overwhelming and all of our normal coping mechanisms become as useful as a map with no place names.

Recently, something horrible happened that completely blind-sided me. At first, I went on to some weird kind of *I-can-handle-this* autopilot.

But then tiredness took over and the light of hope began to fade. All I could see was a creeping, smothering darkness, threatening to swallow me whole.

I pride myself on being a 'coper' and a 'do-er'.

When things go wrong, I instantly want to fix them.

But sometimes we have to accept that we're not superhuman.

We can't fix everything - *and that's OK*!

Sometimes we have to allow ourselves to fall into the human safety net our closest friends and family provide.

Because your closest friends, to paraphrase Elbert Hubbard, *"know all about you and still love you"*, you are able to show them your weakness and vulnerability without fear.

These friends never judge you. They never try to capitalise on your pain. You can stand in front of these friends, weeping and emotionally naked, and they don't shirk from your scars. In fact they want to help heal them.

In the past week my closest friends and family have woven a safety net around me made from texts and phone calls and Skype calls and emails.

I've been sent advice and inspiration and jokes and chocolate.

I've been surrounded and held by love.

There's something so incredibly healing about being loved and supported in this way. To know that these amazing people are your friends despite having seen you at your most vulnerable … not to mention snotty. To know that you can fall and they will catch you, is so comforting.

Today, thanks to my human safety net, I woke up with a renewed sense of hope and optimism. And the knowledge that, whatever challenges the world might throw at me, with friends and family like mine, everything will turn out just fine.

When the Crap Hits the Fan - Build Yourself a Bed Bubble

Sometimes (actually, often, *very* often) I feel as if the world is collectively suffering from some kind of mental illness. I could go on for hours and pages about all of the reasons why but today I want to focus on just one: the elevation of exhaustion to some kind of warped life goal.

When I was a little kid back in the 1970s our teacher would sometimes get us to imagine what the world would be like in THE YEAR 2000!

Back then, THE YEAR 2000! seemed such a long way off it had sci-fi proportions and always had to be spoken about in upper case with an exclamation mark.

And to our seven-year-old selves, we saw THE YEAR 2000! as being some kind of chilled-out utopia where all the crappy stuff, like vacuuming and cooking, oh, and *working*, was done by robots and we all lay around all day watching TVs that HUNG ON THE WALL and having phone conversations WHERE YOU COULD ACTUALLY SEE EACH OTHER'S FACES.

It's now 2015.

Flat-screen TVs hang on walls everywhere and we have Face Time, Google Hangouts and Skype.

But where the hell are the frickin' robots?!

And why the hell are we working longer hours than ever before?

THE YEAR 2000! you have let us down.

Even worse, we've been brainwashed into thinking that bone-achingly busy is a good thing.

We multi-task our way through life like computers with way too many windows open.

And as a result, we become frazzled, anxious and stressed.

I discovered the joys of building myself a bed bubble quite by accident.

One rainy Sunday I was so tired that when my alarm went off, I decided to stay in bed *just a little longer*.

Just a little longer stretched from minutes into hours and hours into the entire morning and the entire morning into the entire day and the entire day into the evening and the evening until it was time to go to bed again. Or in my case, time to *stay* in bed again.

I read books in my bed bubble.

I watched a couple of movies.

But for long stretches of time, I just lay there doing sweet nothing.

It felt incredible.

And so, so indulgent.

I went into the new week feeling refreshed and - when my colleagues started talking about what 'super-busy' weekends they'd had - like a proper rebel.

So, next time you're feeling frazzled, build yourself a bed bubble using the tips below:

- Don't go online - the last thing you want is to lose hours and the will to live, lost down the Facebook Rabbit Hole
- Have a supply of inspirational reads by your bed
- Ditto, tasty snacks
- Turn your phone off - the bed bubble ceases to be healing if you have the ding of notifications constantly piercing the calm
- Watch an inspirational movie (my top recommends are *Eat, Pray Love* and *Under a Tuscan Sky*)
- Don't be afraid to just lie there in silence - embrace the nothingness and make room in your mind for inspiration to strike

A Life of Loving Abundance

When I was training to become a life coach, one of the key modules we covered was Financial Abundance.

Many people have coaching because they wish to become more financially abundant. As coaches we had to be sure that we knew how best to advise them.

'Often, we grow up with limiting beliefs around money,' our trainer told us. 'If our parents had issues with wealth we can subconsciously absorb them.' She then asked us to jot down any limiting beliefs around money we thought might have inherited from our parents.

Hmm.

Most weekends when I was a kid my dad would take my siblings and me out for a walk. Usually this walk would be a circuit of our local parks but sometimes it would be up 'The Hill'.

We lived in a small house on a council estate in North West London (think the Projects, US readers). This council estate was at the bottom of a hill. The top of the hill was like a whole other world. A world of gated driveways and sculpted gardens and sky blue swimming pools. Whenever our dad took us up the hill he would come to a standstill outside a random house and ask: 'Who lives in there?'

We would gaze solemnly at the house in question, a house so big you couldn't even count the gleaming windows, and answer, 'Rich people.'

'And what are rich people?' Our trade unionist dad would say.

'Robbers and parasites,' we'd chorus back as we'd been trained, not really sure what a parasite was but certain it was something really, really bad.

When I relayed this tale to my coaching trainer she looked horrified. Like, if I wasn't already a grown woman she'd have been on the phone to *Childline*, horrified.

Remembering what my dad had done had made me laugh. But later I pondered my coaching trainer's words.

The truth was, having grown up in the midst of such financial extremes, with friends who'd often had to go to bed without dinner because their kitchen cupboards were bare, left me with an uneasy feeling when it came to wealth.

Was the latent negativity I associated with having money the reason I found myself almost permanently in debt?

I tried repeating ra-ra affirmations, such as, '*Wealth is good*'.

I tried seeing my dad as being wrong.

I tried reading books by billionaires about their wealth-building secrets, but in the end I didn't experience a financial breakthrough until I moved my focus from money to love.

I'm aware that this might sound incredibly cheesy-hippy but please resist the urge to picture me sitting cross-legged in a kaftan humming *Kumbaya* and stay with me.

Once I'd developed a spiritual practice and come to the conclusion that the only thing that really counts in life is love, everything else fell into place, including my finances.

When I put love at the heart of what I did, things really took off for me.

When I began focusing on all that I already had, instead of what I lacked, and feeling grateful every day, more seemed to flow into my life.

And when I started to give, I received way more too.

Now when I'm coaching people who are experiencing lack in their lives, I ask them to use the following questions as prompts to change their thinking around money:

- *What are you grateful for right now?*
- *How could you put love at the heart of your work?*
- *What are you able to give right now and to who?*

If you're experiencing financial worries, try free-writing your answers to these questions in a notebook. Don't censor yourself, just see what comes.

Make this a daily practice as I have and see your life fill with abundance.

Love Online

There's no denying that the online world has revolutionised our lives. We can shop with just the click of a button (hello, Amazon overdraft). We can find love with the swipe of a screen. We can watch entire boxsets from just about anywhere.

The internet allows us to connect with the rest of the world, learn about *everything* and even start revolutions, but it comes with a dark side too.

The internet makes a lot of things easier and unfortunately, that includes hate.

According to a recent report, nearly 43% of young people have been victims of cyber bullying.

70% of young people report seeing frequent bullying online.

And 68% of teens think that cyber bullying is a serious issue.

It is a serious issue.

Lives are being ruined and in some tragic cases, ended, because of online haters.

Sometimes I'm asked to run workshops about writing online.

Although I focus mainly on blogging, I also talk about social media and I give the participants this simple guideline to use before posting anything online:

Ask yourself, how will this tweet or update make the reader feel?

If the answer isn't: ***uplifted / inspired / informed / happy*** then don't post.

If you're genuinely angry with someone, don't lash out online, speak to them in person. And if you can't speak to them in person because you don't know them, that's even more reason not to post.

A while ago, a well-known Twitter wind-up merchant posted something crass and heartless about someone who'd just died.

I was so incensed I sent her a tweet, telling her I wasn't sure how she could sleep at night.

But, after I sent it, I was the one unable to sleep.

I'd never done anything like that before, calling a complete stranger out online and it felt wrong.

How did I know what was really going on for this woman? Clearly something wasn't right for her to lash out in the way she did. It was none of my business to get involved.

I got up and deleted the tweet. Only then was I able to sleep.

There's so much hate in the world already.

Let's not add to it, just because the internet makes it easy.

Let's keep on adding to the love and the joy, one tweet and update at a time.

Dare to Love - and Lose

(When the Dare to Dream blog was awarded Top Ten Blog for Dating Courage by Dating Advice.com, this post was singled out for a special mention. As it's probably one of the most heartfelt and personal posts I've ever written, it was lovely to get this recognition...)

I was fifteen years old when I closed myself off to love.

My mum had just told me that she was leaving my dad and moving out.

The night before she left I lay in my bed feeling sick with pain and fear. Part of me wanted to run into her room, tell her I loved her and beg her not to leave.

But I stayed where I was.

I didn't go to her.

I didn't tell her that I loved her.

I didn't beg her not to leave.

I still have such vivid memories of that night. And I can still recall the physical sensation of shutters going up around my heart.

In the midst of my shock and sorrow, I can remember thinking to myself that I must never allow this to happen to me again.

I must never trust someone so utterly and completely with my love - because if they left me too I would be destroyed.

Although I went on to fall in love and have serious relationships with men, my love for them was always tainted with a morbid fear that they would one day leave.

And so, on some level, I always remained guarded. I was always mentally prepared for the worst. I always held a part of me back, just in case.

I thought it would make me feel safe.

It didn't.

And then I went on my Quest to Find True Love - and I found and experienced a deep, spiritual love - and realised that actually, we are very wrong to compartmentalise love in the way we do.

The only true love is unconditional love.

And, in my experience, we can only experience true happiness when we love unconditionally in all areas of our life.

The greatest gift my life has given me is the unconditional love I feel for my son.

But I had been missing out on so much by letting fear have such an influence on my romantic relationships.

Then this year, I was given the opportunity to put all that I had learnt about love into practise.

Right when I was least expecting it, and certainly wasn't looking for it, I met a man.

Instantly, I felt a powerful connection to him - a sense that we were definitely supposed to meet.

And instead of feeling guarded, I opened right up, right away.

In his brilliant book, *Loveability*, Robert Holden talks about how unconditional love between two people creates a space where it is totally safe to be yourself.

For the first time in my life, this is exactly how I felt - safe to be myself, without any fear of being judged or made to feel stupid.

I felt no need to put on any kind of act or pretence in order to protect myself.

I could just be me.

And let me tell you, when you are loved for just being you, there is no finer feeling.

And when another person shows you their truth and their vulnerability - when they allow you to really see them for who they are and love them for who they are - it is a beautiful experience.

It's like watching a flower bloom.

But of course it's all very well loving unconditionally when life takes on the soft focus glow of a rom-com montage. The real test is if the relationship ends.

Recently, my relationship with this man finished.

The ending was unexpected, unforseen and brutal in its swiftness.

It left me feeling physically bereft.

My worst nightmare had come true.

I had finally opened myself up to love completely and I had lost him. But the strangest thing happened.

Rather than drowning in self-pity or bitterness; rather than telling myself, '*I told you so!*'; rather than putting up all of my defences again, I just opened my heart even wider.

This is another thing I've learnt - when you love a person unconditionally, you feel no sense of possession over them. You have no demands. It becomes all about the giving, not the taking.

Even if that means giving them your love and blessing when they leave.

And in the relatively brief period of time we were together, I was given so much.

So, even though I'm still feeling the loss of his physical presence in my life acutely and my first instinct would be to describe that feeling as being broken-hearted, that would be wrong. Because my heart isn't 'broken' at all.

When you share unconditional love with another, your heart expands, grows wings and flies.

And even if that person leaves, their love remains imprinted on your heart forever - glowing like stars and guiding you through the darkness of loss to the light of happier times to come.

Even after all this time,
The sun never says to the earth:
'You owe me!'
Look what happens with
A love like that!
It lights the whole sky!
Hafiz

This Solstice, Love Like the Sun

It's the summer solstice, and here in the UK it is one of those beautiful clear sunny days where the whole world looks as if it's been painted in water colours.

Even if it isn't sunny where you are, today is the perfect opportunity to take inspiration from the solstice and expand your capacity to give and receive light and love.

So with that in mind, I've come up with a little solstice meditation for you.

First, find a time when you won't be interrupted (to do this properly you'll need at least 20 minutes).

Turn off your phone and come off-line (controversial I know, but for you to get the maximum benefit from this you mustn't have any distractions).

Sit upright in silence for a few moments, just focusing on your breathing: *in through the nose, and out through the mouth, slowly and gently.*

As you focus on your breathing, try to relax your body and let go of any mental chatter in your mind.

Once you feel fully present, take a moment to reflect upon the first half of this year.

Think of all the things you're proud of achieving: in your work life, in your home life, in your relationships, and within yourself.

Jot these things down in a notebook.

Think of all the challenges you've faced so far this year.

Feel proud of how you've dealt with them and write them down.

Now sit back and look at your list.

Acknowledge all that you've done.

Really acknowledge it.

Life today is so crazy-fast.

We're always striving, always driving ourselves forwards.

Today, mentally pull over and see how far you've come.

As you're acknowledging yourself and your achievements, feel yourself surrounded by love and light.

Close your eyes and visualise that love and light filling your body.

See yourself shining as brightly as the sun.

Then picture the people you love.

Visualise love and light pouring from your heart into theirs, until they are as full of love as you are.

Then finally, picture anyone who has caused you stress or pain this year.

Visualise light and love pouring from you into them and see how healing it feels to let go of anger, pain and fear and how empowering it is to simply love.

This last stage is the hardest but usually provides the biggest breakthrough.

If it makes you cry allow yourself to cry as they will be cleansing tears.

Keep repeating the process until you feel empty of pain and full of love.

Wishing you a summer filled with love and light.

Tip: There's a beautiful song by Snatam Kaur called *Longtime Sun* that works perfectly as a soundtrack for this solstice meditation. You can find it on YouTube.

Live, Love and Laugh Like a Child

Today I wanted to write a blog about self-loathing and how it can so often sabotage our happiness.

But as I sat down to write, this poem popped out instead.

SOMETIMES

Sometimes...
I look in the mirror and all I see is fat

Sometimes...
I hear myself speaking and it makes me cringe

Sometimes...
I read my work and shame seeps through my skin

Sometimes...
I take the words 'he doesn't love you' and add 'nobody can'

Sometimes...
I hate myself

But sometimes . . .

Sometimes...
I dance in the street with flowers in my hair

Sometimes...
I hear my son's laughter and it makes my heart soar

Sometimes...
I run through a meadow, wild as a horse

Sometimes...
I buy the biggest cake and eat the icing first

Sometimes...
I climb a tree, just to see how a bird must feel

Sometimes...
I look into a man's eyes and see the glow of God

Sometimes...
I sit. In silence. And just be.

And those times - every time
I am filled with Love.

Why are us humans so prone to self-loathing?

Why, when we look in the mirror, do we instantly zoom in on our so-called flaws?

Why do we cringe at some of the things we say and do?

Why do we sometimes believe ourselves to be unworthy of love?

Self-loathing can be such an automatic reflex I think most of us don't even stop to question it.

We see our bitchy inner commentary as the truth.

But is it really?

Take a moment to think of the most common ways in which you put yourself down.

If you can, jot them down on a piece of paper.

Get them all out - leave no moan unturned!

How are you harsh on yourself over your appearance, your work, your interactions with others, your loveability?

Now take a good look at your list and ask yourself if you would ever say such things to a friend or loved one.

Unless you are the friend or loved one from hell, my guess is that you wouldn't dream of it.

So why is it okay to talk to yourself in this way?

Having spent most of last night pondering this, here are my conclusions:

- As humans we have an innate need to be loved and belong.

- This can make us paranoid about not fitting in - about not looking or acting in a way that is acceptable to the rest of the pack ie; society.

- And so we scrutinise ourselves for any possible shortcomings - anything that could lead to us being mocked or ostracised.

- We do this out of fear.

- Fear of rejection.

- Fear of hurt.

- When we tell ourselves we aren't loveable we are really trying to stop ourselves from opening up to love.

- We are really thinking, *love is scary, love hurts when they don't love us back, but if I accept that I'm not loveable to begin with, I can avoid that pain.*

- The irony is, by telling ourselves we're unloveable, we are hurting ourselves from the outset, and blocking any potential future joy.

Have you noticed that young children are completely free from self-loathing?

Young children simply live in the moment - and treat every moment as an opportunity to play.

They see a puddle and they splash.

They see a tree and they climb.

They hear music and they dance.

They aren't concerned with what they look like or how they'll be judged.

They just throw themselves at life, laughing and singing.

And this, I think, is the answer.

We need to learn from children.

As came through in my poem, whenever I live life as fearlessly and imaginatively as a child I'm filled with joy and love.

And I'm far too busy having fun to worry about what I look like or what others might think of me.

Instead of dulling myself down with self-criticism, I allow my individuality to shine.

And so should you.

For the rest of this week - for the rest of this *lifetime* - dare to throw yourself at life, dancing and singing, and live, laugh and love like a child.

In Memory of 9/11: The Love That Unites

Today is the twelfth anniversary of 9/11.

It's so hard not to think of what happened on that day without the word 'terror' entering your mind:

'Terrorist attack'

'War on Terror'

'Terrorist atrocity'

'Terror victims'

These are just some of the terror-based phrases forever linked to what happened twelve years ago.

I've written a lot about fear on this blog - but always from an individual, rather than collective, point of view.

I've talked about how we can face our fears and overcome them.

And I've talked about how we always have a choice.

We can choose to be fearful...

... or we can choose to love.

Then today, I came across this quote from an American firefighter who was involved in the rescue operation at the Twin Towers:

"9/11 to me is not about terror, it is about the unmistakable and undeniable love that unites us all when we no longer are focused on those ideas that divide us. Responders entering those towers on 9/11 were not American. They were human. They did not help

other Americans, they helped people. They did not check voter
registration cards, or immigration status, or the bank statements
of those they were there to help. Your burka was irrelevant, your
crucifix meaningless."

When I read this, it made my heart sing.

A voice of love and unity, cutting through all of the fear and hate.

I've studied many of the different world religions and the one thing that inspires both hope and despair in me is the fact that most of them boil down to love.

Selfless, unconditional love.

And yet...

Twelve years on from 9/11, the world is polarising over the latest terrorist atrocity - this time in Syria.

It's so hard not to retreat into a place of fear when you're confronted by the slaughter of thousands of innocents.

It's so hard not to seek security in your own set of beliefs.

It's so hard to 'focus on the love that unites us' rather than the 'ideas that divide us'.

But don't we owe it to the millions of innocent people who have died in the name of religion or ideology to at least try?

Is it so impossible for us to connect with the love inside each other?

Must we always focus on being right rather than being love?

Last night I asked my son why he didn't believe in God.

He looked at me with an expression of horror that I should even ask such a question.

My son is an intelligent and deeply caring person.

But to him, and so many of his generation, religion + God = discrimination + hate.

Don't we owe it to our children to set a better example?

Isn't it time we stripped away all dogma and doctrine and started again?

Isn't it time we returned to Love?

Love without racial prejudice.

Love without sexual discrimination.

Love without power.

Love without creed.

Love without condition.

The Love that unites. Everyone.

Je Suis Charlie, Je Suis Ahmed ... Je Suis Human

When the news broke about the shootings at Charlie Hebdo my first reaction was one of horror and sorrow.

And when I heard that my French publisher had been told to evacuate their building as they may also be a target of the gunmen it all felt dangerously close to home.

And pretty soon my sorrow was souring into anger.

Words like *barbaric* and *evil* filled my mind.

The situation in France escalated.

Hostages were taken. More lives were lost. The streets of Paris teemed with armed police. I watched the live news feed with a growing sense of dread and fear.

We Will Be Next! the headlines in the UK screamed.

A plague of anti-Muslim tweets spread across Twitter.

And then I came across this quote from Gandhi:

"If love is not the law of our being, the whole of my argument falls to pieces. I know that without an intelligent return to simplicity, there is no escape from our descent to a state lower than brutality."

The words '*love*' and '*simplicity*' cut straight through my tangled thoughts of anger and fear. And I realised that I shouldn't just be proclaiming to be Charlie on my social media accounts, I should be proclaiming to be Ahmed Merabet, the Muslim policeman who died defending the offices of Charlie Hebdo, too. I realised that I - and we all – should be proclaiming to be human.

It seems clear to me now that the only way out of this descent into madness and destruction is to focus on our shared humanity.

And to ask why, *to really ask why*, this is happening.

The attack on Charlie Hebdo wasn't a random, completely out of the blue attack on the freedom of speech, it goes far deeper than that.

And by asking why it happened we need to be prepared for some uncomfortable answers.

Over Christmas I read '*I Am Malala*' by Malala Yousafzai, the teenage girl shot by the Taliban for her courageous campaigning for girls' education.

In her book, Malala describes the fear of living in Pakistan when the Western drone strikes began. It made me stop and think about how terrifying it must be to live in a place where a bomb could drop out of the sky on you at any moment.

The painful truth of the matter is that drone strikes don't just kill their terrorist targets, they kill innocent civilians too.

Not all people are strong enough to live in such fearful conditions and not end up wanting to seek revenge - as was witnessed this week in the wave of retaliation attacks upon French Muslims.

This cycle of fear and revenge needs to be broken. And the only way this can be done is if enough of us come together and yell from the rooftops, 'not in our name'.

Just like the vast majority of Muslims, I don't want innocent people being killed in my name.

I truly believe that the vast majority of us want to live together in peace.

But we'll never achieve that peace by bombing and shooting each other. How can we?

Yesterday, in amongst all of the terrible news stories coming out of Paris, I came across a little-reported story of a group of British Muslims who had 'love-bombed' the French embassy in London, posting messages of love and support on the wall.

Then I read an article by Ali Gokal and I felt hopeful again, particularly at this:

"The Prophet Muhammad's cousin Ali ibn Abu Talib encapsulated Islamic teaching of tolerance when he said "a person is either your brother in faith or your equal in humanity". And the Prophet himself said: "Injustice is regarded as one of the greatest sins. Therefore, oppressing people because they have different beliefs is rejected."

I also realised that if I want peace I can't just sit at home watching the news and wringing my hands.

I have to work for it.

We all do.

By asking uncomfortable questions. By educating ourselves. By finding our shared humanity.

By making love, not fear, the law of our being.

Choose Love and Courage

The average person makes 612 choices per day.

Which works out at around 4,900 choices per week, and 254,800 per year.

Them's a lot of choices!

And it is through these choices that we build our lives.

Of course, not all choices are voluntary.

If some eejit pulls out in front of you at a crossroads, you don't waste precious seconds pondering whether or not to stop. Your brain sends a signal to your foot in no uncertain terms to *press the damn brake pedal already!*

But a lot of the 600+ choices we make each and every day are voluntary.

Whether it be to have peanut butter on our toast, paint the living room purple, take the job, or end the relationship, our choices big and small form the DNA of our daily lives.

And this would all be fine and dandy if we always made the 'right' choices.

If our choices were always coming from a place of certainty and authenticity.

But how often do we make choices from a place of fear?

Take a moment to reflect upon your life.

Which choices do you regret making?

Now dig a little deeper and try to unearth the emotion behind each choice.

And ask yourself, were you choosing out of fear?

The friendship you regret ending...

The job you regret taking...

The opportunity you wish you hadn't ignored...

The person you wish you'd taken the time to get to know...

Examine the motives behind those choices you regret making.

And learn from them.

Realise that whenever you let fear influence the choices you make in your life, you usually live to regret it.

Now think about the choices you've made that make your heart sing:

The person you chose to get to know better who ended up becoming the love of your life...

The job you took that ended up teaching you so much...

The new town or country you moved to that ended up becoming your spiritual home...

The risk you chose to take that led to you embarking upon an inspiring and empowering adventure...

Now dig deeper and uncover the driving emotions behind these choices.

And learn from them too.

Every time you make a choice from a place of courage and love, you cannot fail to grow.

Even if the choice doesn't lead to the desired outcome, the simple act of being loving and/or brave will have helped to make you stronger.

Whereas choosing from a place of fear causes you to shrink.

So as you go about your life, hopping from one choice to the next, always remember to let love and courage be your guide.

How to Love Your Way to a Happy Christmas

'Tis the season to be jolly, tra-la-la-la-la-la-la-la-la' ... but Christmas can have its fair share of trials and tribulations too. So I wanted to write this post for anyone who might be struggling a bit this Christmas.

Anyone who has lost someone this year.
Anyone who is on their own.
Anyone who is having financial difficulties.
Anyone who is apprehensive about spending 'quality time' with certain family members.

And as I thought about what I'd advise in each of these situations, I realised that the answer was the same. A simple four-letter word. *(No, not that one - although said at certain key times it can definitely be therapeutic!)*

I realised that LOVE can help transform every single Christmas hazard into happiness. Here's how...

If you've lost someone and you're dreading your first Christmas without them ... let your love for them melt away the pain.

Take some time, this Christmas, to honour their memory, to celebrate their life, to send them love. Write them a Christmas card telling them how much you miss them and listing all the ways in which they changed your life for the better. Buy them a present; a donation to their favourite charity, some flowers in their favourite colour, a candle to light in their memory.

If you're on your own this Christmas ... let love for yourself and others chase away the loneliness.

With so much emphasis placed on families and couples at this time of year, the prospect of Christmas on your own can be really depressing. You picture the rest of the world, all hugging by the Christmas tree and soft-focus smooching beneath the mistletoe and you feel like a big fat Christmas failure. But this is all an optical illusion. For a start, many, many couples find Christmas together a pain worse than root canal - hence the dramatic upsurge in divorce proceedings every January. And for lots of families, far from being jolly, Christmas 'tis the season for aggravating old wounds and grievances - *more on which, later.* Being single and having no ties at Christmas can actually be a real blessing. *If you choose to see it as such.* It's the perfect time to pause and take stock; to focus on all you've achieved. It's the perfect time to dream-weave by candle-light, getting clear on the adventures you want to invite into your life in the coming year. It's the perfect time to snuggle down and watch the movies of your choice. It's the perfect time to read a good book. Or three. And to eat whatever the hell you want. It's the perfect time to show yourself some love. Buy yourself a gift from the heart. Write yourself a card, listing five things you're really proud of. Sign it with 'lots of love' and tons of meaning. Find love in your heart for some of the countless people facing a real crisis this Christmas. Donate some gifts or time to your local foodbank. Volunteer at a soup kitchen. The year her marriage broke up, a friend of mine volunteered for a homeless charity over Christmas. Afterwards she spoke so movingly about how it had helped her; teaching her the importance of giving and the true meaning of Christmas. In giving to others we also give to ourselves and chase away all feeling of loneliness.

If you're struggling financially this Christmas ... give your love for free.

Somewhere along the line, Christmas has become an orgy of consumerism and if you're struggling financially, this can cause untold pressure and stress. But it doesn't have to be like this. I'll never forget the horrified expression on my son's face When I told him what Christmas was like when I was little. How we'd get satsumas and sugar mice in our stockings and advent calendars WITH NO CHOCOLATE. *'Christmas was so bad in the olden days!'* he gasped. But actually it wasn't. I used to get stupidly excited about the pictures hiding behind the advent calendar doors and the sugar mice in my stocking seemed like the most magical gifts on earth - *because they'd been hand-delivered by Father Christmas!* The fact is, the best things in life come without a price tag. And it's amazing the gifts you can create with a lot of love and a sprinkling of imagination. Here are just a few ideas:

Make some 'vouchers' entitling the recipient to a token of your love: *An evening of babysitting. A free lesson in something you're good at. An offer of your shopping / cleaning / gardening services.*

If you're artistic, why not create something for your loved-ones showing them how much they mean to you.

Or hand-make personalised cards, containing a list of reasons why you love the recipient - who wouldn't want to receive a gift like that?

If you're apprehensive about spending Christmas with certain in-laws or family members ... give them the gift of forgiveness and free yourself too.

When you stop to think about it, Christmas contains all the ingredients for potential family carnage:

- *Long periods of time together with no escape*

- *Vast quantities of alcohol*

- *Ditto food*

- *Countless competitive-spirit / sore-loser provoking games*

- *Endless TV*

- *Sahara-hot central heating*

- *Squabbling children*

- *A stressed-out chef*

- *And that weird way in which we all revert to our childhood roles*

Even the strongest of family bonds can be tested to the limit under these conditions. But if you've got a family member you find it hard to get on with at the best of times, Christmas can stretch your patience to breaking point.

But in the spirit of the L-word, why not see this Christmas as the perfect opportunity to forgive?

Forgiveness is love on steroids.

It's easy to love those people in your life who are kind and supportive but to love the ones who make it their life's work to press your buttons, well, that's hard-core indeed. But the best thing about forgiveness is that it makes you feel brilliant. There's a famous saying:

Not forgiving someone is like drinking poison and hoping they'll die.

I'd like to give that quote a seasonal tweak: *Not forgiving someone is like watching the EastEnders* Christmas Special and hoping they'll be the one to jump out of the window in despair. (*For non-UK readers, EastEnders is an ultra-bleak TV soap and their Christmas Special usually involves at least one murder, drugs overdose and marriage break-up)* You don't need to tell the person concerned that you forgive them - you just need to tell yourself - and really mean it.

Write the person a letter you'll never send. Get any residual anger off your chest, then ask yourself how you could see them in a more loving light. Try to find compassion and understanding for why they are the way they are. Finish your letter by sending them love. Sit in peace and quiet for a while. Visualise your Christmas Button-Pusher sitting in front of you. Picture love radiating from you into them like golden sunlight. Allow it to melt away your feelings of stress and resentment. Figure out a coping strategy for if the crap does hit the fan. If they say or do something that really winds you up, how could you deal with it in a non-confrontational way? How could you stay cool and calm and full of love? *(Top tip: try feeling sorry for them.)* And remember, forgiving them doesn't make you a walkover or weak, it makes you incredibly strong. By loving the people who wind us up we make life infinitely easier for ourselves.

And finally...

Whatever you're doing this Christmas and whoever you're with, keep LOVE as your motto and peace and joy won't be far behind.

If You Can't be With the Work You Love … Love the Work You're With

Most of us spend more of our waking hours at work than we do with our loved ones.

When I first realised this fact it caused me to almost keel over in horror.

At the time I was working in an office where the clock went backwards - at least the work was so dull and unrewarding it seemed that way.

I also had the boss from hell - a woman named May, who was so cold and bitter she really ought to have been renamed February. It was the middle of a recession and I'd dropped out of uni, so rewarding and interesting jobs were thin on the ground. But some of my most fun memories are from the two years I worked in that office.

The job was hell, the boss was a tyrant, the clock went backwards, but my colleagues and I banded together and somehow made it a pleasant place to work.

We played pranks on one and another, we embarked on crazy pub-dashes during our *half hour* lunch break (the only time of the day when the office clock went forwards). We formed a social club and went on trips to comedy clubs and night clubs and even France.

Sometimes we have to do jobs that are dull, unfulfilling and stressful but because we spend so much time at work, it's vital we find a way to make it a positive experience. Listed below are some of the most common complaints I've had from coaching clients regarding their jobs, and what I've advised they do to try and stay sane.

'I don't get on with my boss / colleague...'

If you don't get on with a colleague or boss it's all too easy to let this grow into a full-blown obsessive hatred of the *Sunday-evening-spent-sticking-pins-in-their-effigy* variety. This is very bad because now they're not just getting to you when you're at work, but when you're at home too. A simple way of letting go of the stress they cause you is through compassion. I once had a boss who was the walking, shouting, sneering definition of the word bully. She got a kick out of putting people down and on several occasions she made members of her staff cry. It used to really get to me until I took a step back. For a grown woman to need to belittle her employees like this there had to be something very wrong in her life; she had to be deeply unhappy. Once I'd made that realisation every time she made a snide remark I wouldn't see a scary woman, I'd see a frightened little girl acting up and I'd shake her comments off. Interestingly, when I stopped being affected by her putdowns, she stopped putting me down. Bullies need a reaction to get their kicks. Don't give them one.

'My co-workers love to bitch but it brings me down...'

Workplaces can all too easily become hotbeds of hatred - especially if the work is tedious and unfulfilling. A good old gossip session can relieve the tedium by creating some much-needed drama but the trouble is, it leaves you feeling grubby. And if there's a culture of bitching and back-stabbing, you always have the insecurity of wondering if you're a victim of it too. The best policy when it comes to gossip is to not engage. Be fun and chatty and a positive member of the team but the moment the bitching starts, discreetly withdraw from the fray. After a while people will start to notice and your silence may well get them to question their own behaviour. Even if it doesn't, you will feel a whole lot better about yourself.

'This isn't what I want to be doing with my life...'

This is probably the most common of all the workplace complaints and often the reason people come for coaching. As I know all too well, it's so easy to lose sight of your career dreams, or for dreaded RESPONSIBILITIES to get in the way. The best way to get over this and to stop resentment ruining your work-life is to start plotting your escape *and to see your current job as a help rather than a hindrance in this process.*

For many years as a single mum, I had to work in less than fulfilling jobs to keep a roof over our heads. But all the while, I was building my dream career as a writer and coach alongside. It was tiring - exhausting even - but it paid off. And any time I felt the bitter bite of resentment as I got up at the crack of dawn to set off for my London job, I'd remind myself that this job wasn't keeping me from my dream, it was *funding* it. A vital distinction and one that made me full of gratitude instead of regret.

Single, Sassy, Fearless and Free

Recently, I bumped into an old acquaintance. We hadn't seen each other in a while so naturally our conversation began with, *'How are you? What's new?'*

She told me all about the latest row she'd had with her partner. She also told me about the anxiety attacks she frequently experiences.

Sadly, I can't help thinking that these two facts are linked. Her partner is extremely controlling and likes to dictate every aspect of her life - right down to the clothes she wears to do the gardening.

When she asked me what was new in my life I told her how I was launching a *Dare to Dream* publishing imprint and how excited I was to have some new books coming out soon. I told her that my son was doing well in school and all was good at home. I also told her that next year, I hope to do some travelling in America and India. 'That's nice,' she said, blankly. 'But what about on the romantic front. *Any man news?*'

When I told her I was single it was as if I'd said I only had two months to live. Her eyes filled with pity and she actually said, 'Oh dear.'

But there's nothing 'oh dear' about being single.

Nothing at all.

It's just that in our Noah's Ark style, two-by-two society, we're conditioned to believe that there's something missing or something wrong with us if we don't have a partner. And this conditioning can cause us to become consumed with self-doubt, sobbing along to *I Will Survive*, eating our body weight in Ben & Jerry's etc, etc.

So instead of dancing through life embracing the adventure, we limp along feeling unworthy and ashamed.

The other day I went out to lunch with some of my closest girlfriends. There were seven of us around the table and half way through the meal, it dawned on me that every one of us is currently single. But we weren't sobbing into our tenth dessert, shaking our heads and saying 'oh dear'. We were too busy talking about our work and our dreams and passions. We were too busy planning our next adventures. And laughing our heads off. There was so much love around that table. There is so much love in my life.

My single status doesn't make me feel bereft of love.

It makes me feel **sassy** and **fearless** and **free**.

But there was a time when I never would have been able to say that - let alone write it in a book. There was a time when I too believed that being single = 'oh dear'. So if you're currently single and it's making you feel sad, try pondering the following questions:

Does not having a partner make you feel bad about yourself? If so, how and why?

How could you change this for the better without finding a partner? For instance, if being single makes you feel unattractive or unworthy, how could you help yourself feel attractive and worthy?

Becoming responsible for your own happiness is one of the most empowering things you can learn to do.

If not having a partner makes you feel sad because you feel it leaves a massive gap in your life, how could you begin filling that gap yourself?

How does being single free you up to pursue certain dreams?

It could be that it gives you the time and space needed to set up your own business.

It could be that it gives you the opportunity to travel to parts of the world that you really want to see.

It could be that it provides you with the chance to pursue a passion, such as amateur dramatics or music or dancing.

Being in love is lovely.

But romantic love can't be forced.

The vast majority of us are always going to have periods in our lives when we aren't in love with another human being.

But we always have the opportunity to fall in love with our lives.

We always have the opportunity to fill our lives with love.

This Valentine's Day, Fall Madly in Love With Life

I used to hate Valentine's Day.

Whether I was single or crazy in love, it seemed so crass and commercialised, I'd always try and block it out.

There was something so depressing about being guilt-tripped by companies like Hallmark into being loving.

Roses are red,

Violets are blue,

If you don't buy this card,

There's something wrong with you.

If you've ever seen a couple trapped in sullen, silent hell at a Valentine's Day restaurant table then you'll know exactly what I'm talking about!

Love should never be forced.

It should never be about buying each other cards and gifts *because we feel we ought to*.

And our self-worth should never be measured by how many cards in red envelopes the postman delivers.

But then I experienced a Valentine's Day like no other and it changed my whole perspective.

My partner at the time had just been diagnosed with an

extremely virulent form of cancer. He'd just had major surgery to remove a tumour from his brain.

He'd just been told he probably only had months to live.

We spent that Valentine's Day in bed.

Not in *that* way. My partner was still recovering from the surgery. He was barely able to walk. But somehow he managed to sneak out to buy me a Valentine's card.

And there was so much true love contained within the words in that card, I will treasure it forever.

As we lay there, snuggled in our temporary cocoon, protected from the rest of the world, I realised with crystal clarity how much I loved this man. And how much I loved this life.

When death comes calling, it is terrifying, heart-breaking and gut-wrenching, but it also brings a liberating sense of perspective.

So now, every Valentine's Day, I celebrate my love for life and everyone in it.

If Valentine's Day has been leaving you cold, try any or all of the following to help you celebrate your love for life too:

- Send cards to your most treasured friends, telling them why you love them.

- Play songs that uplift and inspire you and remind you of happy times. The tune that was playing during that sun-drenched holiday, the ballad that reminds you of your sweetest love.

- Take part in the One Billion Rising campaign and join women all over the world, dancing for love and justice.

- Write a love letter to life, thanking it for all the gifts it has given you.

- Spread the love by carrying out a random act of kindness.

- Give yourself the perfect gift of self-love. Woo yourself, take yourself on a date, remind yourself of all you have achieved and all the reasons you have to feel proud.

My former partner defied the doctors and all the odds.

He has now been cancer-free for over five years.

We're not exactly sure how he did it - but I'd like to think at least part of it was down to love.

Be a Channel for Love

This morning when I was out walking, I met a man making wood-carvings on his boat.

I asked him how he got the ideas for his creations.

'The wood tells me what it wants to be,' he replied. *'All I have to do is listen.'*

As I took a look around I saw a predominance of heart-shaped carvings on the deck.

'It seems to be all about love at the moment,' he said with a chuckle. *'But I think that's a good thing - there's far too much fighting and hatred in the world right now.'*

As I walked on, I couldn't get his words out of my head.

And it got me thinking.

Surely the wood is symbolic of this planet.

Surely all Mother Earth wants is for us to be channels for love.

If only we would all just stop... *stop fighting and fearing and judging and sneering* ... and listen.

A Musing on Love

And in the end, it was simple:

Love never leaves.

Ponder this musing for a moment.

How is it true in your life?

How can you gain comfort from it?

How has love stayed with you long after a person has left?

Part Three: Creativity

"An essential aspect of creativity is not being afraid to fail."

Edwin Land

Dear Dare to Dream: How Can I Find the Courage to Record My Songs?

Dear Dare to Dream,

At Christmas in 2012, around the time when we were all sarcastically afraid of apocalyptic Mayan prophecies, I was in a little pub in Weymouth (of all places) writing a bucket list of things I'd like to do should I survive.

On it was to record an album.

Now, I don't want to be the new big thing, I'm not going to put myself at the mercy of X Factor also-rans in order to get a hit. But I do really want to make use of the dozens of songs I've written since I was about eight.

I first started penning ditties by childishly re-writing the lyrics of 80s classics such as *Hungry Like The Wolf* (the shame!) and I went through a really awful phase of writing soppy love songs in my teens (highlights include comparing my love to an onion because it has many layers. The horror!)

But as I've grown up I've created a collection of songs like one collects pieces for a scrapbook - memories and anecdotes that I'd like to record as a kind of memoir. And so that I can say that I've gone and done it after years of thinking about it.

Thing is, I'm scared stiff by the thought of actually doing it in case people don't like it, despite my lack of desire to make it onto the cover of a revived *Smash Hits* or sing on a resuscitated *Top of the Pops*.

Where do I even begin on the path to making music? I can't play an instrument. I balk at the thought of singing in public. I don't know anyone who knows anyone who I could 'collab' with, either as a producer or instrumentalist or both.

And what if the songs I think are good are actually rubbish?

So the years go by and I tell myself one day someone outside will hear me warbling from the bathroom and sign me on the spot (preferably after I've made myself decent). I put an ad on *Gumtree* peddling my wares and a local singer/songwriter did come forward, but I was too anxious to go through with it.

I'm a procrastinator at heart, and a useless dreamer who is afraid that he'll take all of his songs to the grave. Along with his oniony love.

What do you suggest?

Much appreciation,

That Guy.

Dear That Guy,

I don't think there's a person alive who wouldn't instantly relate to your email - whether they want to record an album of songs or not.

The fact is, pursuing our dreams can be really, *really* scary.

I would even go as far as to say that a dream isn't worth pursuing unless it scares the bejaysus out of you.

The dreams that break you out in a cold sweat – and give you nightmares about singing at Wembley to a chorus of boos - are actually the ones that have the power to transform your life for the better and bring untold happiness.

So why do we let fear sabotage them?

Because all dreams worth dreaming contain some element of risk.

In the case of your dream, That Guy, you're risking looking stupid.

'What if my songs are rubbish?' you ask.

And then you quickly build on this fear with layer upon layer of limiting beliefs:

'I can't play an instrument.'

'I balk at singing in public.'

'I don't know anyone I could collaborate with.'

And phew, it's all okay, your dream is on hold, and public humiliation averted.

Except that it's not okay. Because unexplored dreams don't just vanish. They tick away inside of us like unexploded bombs. And they leave us feeling unhappy and frustrated and useless.

Dear That Guy, you are not a 'useless dreamer'. You are a clearly eloquent and passionate dreamer with a chronic case of the heebee-jeebees.

And the good news is, as a former chronic heebee-jeebee sufferer, I have become somewhat of an expert in overcoming fear.

So here's my advice.

First of all, let's shrink your fear a bit.

You say that you balk at singing in public.

I would advise you invest in one singing lesson.

Just one. To see what happens.

I'm betting that what happens is your singing coach gives you a much needed confidence boost, not to mention some expert tips and advice. I'm also betting that it will be a lot of fun.

Once you've treated yourself to a little vocal advice and training it's time to find a musician to collaborate with.

The good news is you've had a practise run at doing this, in that you placed an ad on *Gumtree*. It doesn't matter one bit that you didn't go through with it in the end - at least you know how and where to place an ad. And that people will respond.

Song-writers and musicians take their craft seriously and they love collaborating. They are not out to bring other people down and destroy their confidence. And I know this to be true because I've been in your position.

Once upon a time, I wrote some song lyrics for a novel. I thought it would be nice to bring this song to life, so I asked a musician if he would help me.

We spent the day in Richmond Park, with him strumming his guitar and humming some possible tunes and me adapting my lyrics slightly to fit.

It was one of the most enjoyable creative experiences of my life. And I have no doubt that it would be exactly the same for you too. So, let's picture the scene and visualise the dream.

You place an ad on *Gumtree*.

A local song-writer / muso-type responds.

You meet for a coffee and show them some of your lyrics.

They give you their feedback.

They start humming out a possible tune.

You give them your feedback.

Together, you fine tune the melody to perfectly match your words.

You see your song coming to life; flying from the pages of your song-book in streams of crotchets and quavers.

It feels incredible.

You agree to work together and you record the song.

You don't think it's rubbish.

In fact, you love it.

And this is the most important thing when it comes to creative dreams.

As long as you love what you've created, that's all that counts.

Don't worry about anyone else.

The minute you start creating from a place of fear and trying to fit what you think other people might want, you lose your spark.

When you create purely for the love of it, you fear-proof your dream.

I'd like to end with some wise words from Mark Twain

"Twenty years from now you will be more disappointed by the things that you didn't do than by the ones you did so. So throw off the bowlines. Sail away from the safe harbor. Catch the trade winds in your sails. Explore. Dream. Discover."
The world needs people who explore, dream and discover.

The world needs your songs, That Guy, including your oniony love.

Good luck - and keep me posted...

Siobhan x

How JK Rowling Helped Me Through My Darkest Days as a Writer

I started writing books during a very difficult time in my life.

My marriage had come to a painful and traumatic end and I was single mum to a young son.

It was a very fearful time - I can remember many sleepless nights spent wondering how I was going to make ends meet and keep a roof over our heads.

I also felt like a total failure. Coming from a 'broken home' I had always vowed that I'd never put any child of mine through that trauma.

Apart from my son, the only light in the darkness of those days was my writing.

When I began working on my first novel it provided a welcome escape from the harsh realities of my life at the time.

But my writing itself was not without fear.

I had no previous experience of writing fiction.

I hadn't done any courses in creative writing.

I didn't have any contacts in the publishing world.

I wasn't a member of any writing group.

I had no idea if what I was creating was any good at all - let alone publishable.

I wrote mainly when my son was asleep and there were some nights when I would be slumped over my typewriter (I couldn't even afford a computer!) crying with exhaustion and wondering why the hell I was even bothering.

It was on those nights that one person helped urge me on and gave me just enough hope to keep me typing.

That person was J K Rowling.

Like the rest of the world, I'd read all the stories about how Rowling had penned the first Harry Potter novel in a cafe in Edinburgh as a penniless single mum.

But, rather than merely being a heart-warming anecdote, this story became a life-line for me.

When Rowling talked about her feelings of despair as a single mum I could so relate to her experience.

And the fact that she had kept on working through her dark times; had kept the faith in her creative dream and gone on to achieve such remarkable success, formed a beacon, guiding me through my own doubt and fear.

Last week, I went up to Edinburgh and visited the cafe where J K Rowling had written that first Harry Potter book.

Having played such an important part in my own vision of hope for the future, it was extremely moving to finally be there. And in a really magical way, it proved to be a gift that kept on giving. The past couple of months have been a bit of a tough time for me, in that I've suffered some personal loss and felt a bit demotivated work-wise.

But sitting at a table in the corner of the cafe, picturing J K Rowling writing away and conjuring up such a magical future for herself and so many readers, I felt a wave of optimism and hope wash over me.

Remembering how far I'd come since my own dark days made me feel humbled and excited. It reminded me that anything is possible if you are prepared to work hard and simply *believe*.

Before leaving the cafe I went into the toilets. They were covered from floor to ceiling in graffiti dedicated to J K Rowling from grateful readers.

Once again, I felt a wave of happiness and excitement. It reminded me what a privilege it is to be a writer - and how thrilling it is to be able to affect people's lives for the better with your words. Once again, I felt J K Rowling inspiring and motivating me - and urging me on.

A bit later, I was walking past Waterstones in Edinburgh. I popped inside and headed for the Young Adult section.

When I saw my books there on the shelves it brought tears to my eyes. All those years ago, when I'd sat hunched over my typewriter, with just my love of writing and J K Rowling's example to keep me going, I never would have dreamed that I'd go on to achieve all that I have. And if I can share anything at all with you to help you through your own doubt and fear, it would be this:

Sometimes, in our darkest times, we need a light to guide us. So rather than cower in the shadows of your fear, seek out your light - whether it be in the form of another person, some words of wisdom, or God / the Universe. Let them lead you on, into your own brighter, happier future...

It's Good to be Bad

Today I want to talk about creativity and how, when it comes to creating something, it's okay to do it badly.

In fact - scrap that - it isn't just okay, it's downright bloody brilliant.

Previously, I've written about our inner voice of doom and how it always likes to throw a spanner in the works whenever we're attempting something remotely scary. Well, creating something - whether it be a story, picture, song, cake, business - can be a very scary process indeed, and it's at precisely these moments when it can feel as if our inner voice of doom is bellowing at us through a loud hailer.

'You can't do that!'

'That is rubbish!'

'Oh my God, you'd better never show that to anyone!'

'Delete! Delete! Delete!'

Sound familiar?

So why then, am I telling you that it's okay to be bad at something? Surely that's only going to encourage your good old Inner V of D to get even meaner and shout even louder.

Au contraire, my dear Dare to Dreamer. Let me explain why...

I've previously likened the inner voice of doom to a bully - something that is actually coming from a place of deep fear.

Once upon a time, many years ago, I was playing tennis with a guy who was known for his bullying behaviour. It was meant to be a friendly knock-about, but pretty soon it became apparent to me that he was intent on winning at all costs. One of the ways in which he did this was to aim power shots right at my body. Another was to keep up a sarcastic commentary about my own performance.

After about twenty minutes of this, I decided enough was enough. I didn't stop playing, but I stopped trying to play well and focused instead on playing as badly as I could.

My opponent soon realised what I was up to and it frustrated the hell out of him. After all, how could he claim any sense of achievement, winning against someone who was deliberately smashing the ball into the net and crawling round the court like a snail on valium?

So to get back to the subject of creativity, you completely take the sting out of your inner critic if you refuse to play the game. If you say things to yourself like:

'My writing / picture / song / cake / business plan is going to suck but who cares because at least I'm going to have fun trying.'

By adopting this attitude, you immediately take away your inner critic's power. Like my tennis opponent, they will become bored and no longer want to play.

And once you've got them to shut up, you can get down to the serious business of being messy and having fun - key ingredients for any creative endeavour.

If you don't dare to be bad, you might never be any good.

When I started out as a novelist I didn't really take any risks creatively. I was so scared of being bad that the writing of my first novel was a painstaking process. I would spend ages over each line, then each paragraph, then each page - rewording and restructuring and hitting that frickin' delete button every other second.

I didn't realise back then that you have to allow your ideas to flow and to do that, you have to allow for the possibility that they might not work.

When I decided to relaunch my coaching practice I wrote pages of scribbled ideas about how I could help clients. Some of them are downright bonkers and will never see the light of day but, because I was allowing my thoughts to flow freely, some of them are really original and fun.

And this brings us to the heart of the matter...

Just because you allow yourself to do something badly it does not mean that everything you do will be bad.

And it most definitely does not mean that you have to keep anything you're not happy with. You are allowed to sort the wheat from the chaff.

Getting into a creative flow allows your very best ideas to come up and then, once your creative cup runneth over, you can keep the good stuff and get rid of the bad. (Just like I got rid of the nude bongo dancing from my coaching masterplan *ahem*).

So, to recap:

- Tell your inner critic they can take the day off as you're embracing all things crap

- Make a hand-written sign saying: *Everything I create is crap and that's OK!*

- Place it by your desk / computer / work station

- Take a deep breath and smile

- Enjoy the freedom of no longer caring

- Let your ideas begin to flow

- Don't question them, just let them pour out

- GET MESSY!!

- HAVE FUN!!

- Once you've finished, step away for a while, even if it's just to make a cup of tea or have a quick air guitar session

- Then come back to your creation

- What do you like? What do you love? What would you like to let go of?

- Polish the diamonds and get rid of the dirt

- Simple

Interestingly, the more daring I've become creatively and the more I've risked making terrible mistakes in my novels, like writing one entirely made up of emails, or putting a *gasp* sixty-year-old main character in a book for teens, the better they've been received. So in your next creative endeavour, allow yourself to be breathtakingly bad - and be prepared to be breathtakingly good...

You Are Still a Writer

Sometimes it can feel like the hardest thing in the world to actually sit down and write.

Sometimes it feels as if the whole world is conspiring to stop you putting pen to paper.

And to put it frankly, this can be a real pain in the butt!

Last week, I was coaching a writer. One of her main frustrations was having to juggle so many things she felt as if her writing was being forced on to the back-burner.

I could relate straight away - and I bet so many of you can too. If you need to earn a living, go to school or college, or bring up a family, it can be exhausting trying to write as well.

And so sometimes you give up trying.

But if writing is your passion, not being able to write can feel like a part of you - a vital part - is withering away.

And this makes you feel crotchety.

Unhappy.

On edge.

But all is not lost. For those times in your life where you are genuinely too busy or too tired to write, remember this:

You are still a writer.

You still have thinking time.
You can still be plotting and planning in your head.
You can still be growing characters in your imagination.

You can still be jotting ideas down in a notebook.
You can still be allowing a story or poem to percolate.
You can still be using your life experiences as inspiration.
You can still call yourself a writer
Because writing is in your blood.

You are still a writer.

Let Summer Stillness Cure Your Creative Block

"Be still. Stillness reveals the secrets of eternity."
Lao Tzu

Summer has finally arrived in the UK. The sun is shining. The birds are singing. The bees are buzzing. Flip-flops are flip-flopping. Ice-creams are melting. And people are smiling.

One of the things I love most about summer is how it encourages stillness.

The heat slows us, melts us, beckons us outside into nature.

And when we're outside in nature, a magical thing happens...

We become still.

No longer doing.

Or trying.

Or striving.

Or achieving.

Or failing.

Just being...

...still.

Yesterday, instead of pounding away on my computer at my desk, I set up camp in a corner of the garden.

I lay down on a blanket and just watched the clouds drift by.

I listened to the bees as they buzzed around the flowers, and the distant hum of trains passing through the valley.

And I breathed in the sweet scent of honeysuckle mingled with wood-smoke.

At first I felt a few pangs of guilt that I should have been hunched over my desk, working on a new book idea.

But then the strangest thing happened. The more still I became, the more ideas started popping into my head.

Every so often I'd roll onto my side, lazily jot my ideas into my notebook, then roll back to continue cloud-gazing.

By the end of the afternoon I'd done nothing but lie there and yet I had a patchwork of thoughts jotted down - as colourful and vibrant as a bed of roses.

It made me realise that in our rush to keep busy, productive and endlessly achieving, our imaginations can seize up.

If you'll excuse the bathroom metaphor, too much clogging ourselves up with *doing* can lead to a chronic case of creative constipation.

So this summer, take the time to be still.

To smell the flowers.

To watch the clouds.

To listen to the birds.

And to let the whisper of inspiration be heard...

You Have the Right to Write!

A VERY IMPORTANT AND *ahem* OFFICIAL report recently found that often, people will do JUST ABOUT ANYTHING rather than write.

In the report, the following ten things were found to be the favoured forms of procrastination keeping people from putting pen to paper:

1. Spring-cleaning the house

2. Walking the dog - even if you don't have a dog

3. Checking the garden for weeds

4. Checking *next door's* garden for weeds

5. Polishing the skirting boards

6. Clearing out *that* cupboard

7. Taking the contents of *that* cupboard to the dump

8. Staring into space

9. Staring into space whilst wondering what comes *after* infinity

10. Making a cup of tea when you still have one steaming away on your desk

This is one of the great conundrums known to writing-kind (almost as great a conundrum as *what comes after infinity*).

Even when we want to write we become masters at blocking ourselves. But why?

The answer, sweet Dare to Dreamers, is FEAR.

Fear of looking stupid.

Fear of criticism or rejection.

Fear of making ourselves open and vulnerable.

And maybe even fear of success.

But the fact is, writing is one of the best ways of making sense of the world.

It's like breathing for the brain as you sigh your thoughts and feelings on to the page.

And it's one of the most powerful forms of self-expression we have.

We all have the right to write.

Rich or poor.

Young or old.

Educated or uneducated.

So how can we overcome our fears?

You might be familiar with the following quote about how to live a happy life:

'You've got to dance like nobody's watching. Love like you've never been hurt. Sing like nobody's listening and live like it's heaven on earth.'

Well, I'd like to tweak that quote slightly for the purposes of this piece:

'You've got to write like nobody's reading. Write like you've never been hurt. Write like nobody gives a damn and write like the last writer on earth.'

You. Have. The. Right. To. Write.

It's your voice.

Your self-expression.

Your right.

So what if you can't spell and you think a colon is something people with more money than sense irrigate? It's your *voice* that counts - your vision and message.

So what if people criticise or reject what you do? At least you had the guts to do it.

So what if it feels as if you're bleeding your heart all over the page? How can anything heartfelt and authentic ever be 'wrong'?

And so what if someone actually likes what you do - and likes it enough to publish it? So what if this leaves you wide open to potential criticism and hurt on a huge scale?

Your words will have taken on a life of their own. Let them fly free and know that it's impossible to please everybody.

There was a time when I felt too terrified to write.

A time when my skirting boards were so clean you could eat your dinner off them and none of the gardens in my street were troubled by a single weed.

But my need to make sense of the world and pour my heart and soul on to the page won out in the end.

And as soon as I started writing, some of my worst fears were realised.

I had work rejected and criticised.

I wrote things I felt embarrassed about *(article about lucky underpants, anyone?!)*

But I kept going.

Kept writing.

Every day, I faced down my fear and put pen to page.

And today I made the finishing touches to my thirteenth book. So, if you feel the call to write, shove your fear to one side and...

Write like nobody's reading. Write like you've never been hurt. Write like nobody gives a damn and write like the last writer on earth.

Go on - I dare you!

Why Where You Create Affects How You Create

This morning, I was coaching a writer about her book-in-progress and we got to talking about the importance of *where* you write.

One of the luxuries of being a writer is that you can do it pretty much anywhere, but of course it follows that some places are far more conducive to creativity than others.

And what determines this is a very personal thing, unique to each writer.

One time, I tried to do that whole *author-sets-up-camp-in-coffee-shop* routine and I couldn't think straight for the sound of babies crying and businessmen bellowing.

Instead of focusing on my supposed to be heart-warming work-in-progress I became fixated on which would make the most effective gob-stopper - a blueberry muffin or a pain au chocolat.

But other writers I know love that kind of background noise. It feeds their creativity rather than drives them to acts of gagging by cake.

My client this morning had been experiencing a few blocks with her writing, then one day last week, she decided to relocate from her study to her lounge.

'I wanted to make the experience more nurturing,' she explained. *'So I snuggled under a duvet and lit some candles and started tapping away on the laptop.'*

This instantly resonated with me.

Back in January of this year I had two books to write so I needed to drastically up my daily word count. But it was the middle of winter and the downstairs of the cottage I was living in at the time was drafty and cold.

So one day, I decided to write in my much cosier bedroom instead.

And so began one of the most pleasant periods of my writing life.

Every day I'd set my laptop on a pile of cushions, create myself a nest of pillows, light some scented candles and away I'd go.

This new writing post on top of my bed also gave me a stunning view across the valley, which became a great source of inspiration.

I felt snug and secure and relaxed and I guess this freed me up because the words just flowed and flowed.

By the end of March the weather started warming and the world started stirring again.

My books were done and life - and I - moved on.

But the experience stayed with me.

I've since moved house and I have a great little work space at the breakfast bar in my kitchen - which happens to have a direct view through the living room to the high street outside. It's a people-watching paradise.

But whenever I'm feeling blocked, or tired, or in need of a little nurturing, I relocate with my laptop to a pillow nest on my bed.

It works every time.

So next time you sit down to create, ask yourself how you need to feel first.

Do you need to feel nurtured and snug or energised and business-like?

Do you need some soothing peace and quiet? Or do you need a background buzz to give you a lift?

Then pick a location that will inspire that feeling in you and watch your creativity flow...

How Focus Gets Things Finished

So here we are: 2015 laid out before us, as sparkly clean as a brand new Word doc.

And writers everywhere are resolving that this will be *the year.*

The year the novel finally gets written.

The year the poetry collection finally comes together.

The year the screenplay makes it from scribbled index cards to properly formatted script.

The year the short story gets published.

The year the blog gets launched.

And for some writers, all of the above and more may apply.

Some writers have so many goals, their list of writing resolutions is practically a novel in itself.

And while this might initially fire them up with enthusiasm, February tends to find them face down in a bottle of gin, suffering from a chronic case of Resolution Overwhelm.

I know this because there was a time when my own writing resolutions had a higher word count than *War and Peace.*

There were so many things I wanted to write; so many genres and age groups and mediums I wanted to write for.

So I'd list them all.

And then, in January, I'd make a start on them all. And I'd end up spreading my writing so thinly that I'd lose heart.

Nothing ever seemed to get done.

So I'd give up doing it at all.

Then I discovered the clear-headed joy that is prioritising.

And, dear *Dare to Dreamers*, it has revolutionised my life.

Let me show you how...

First, write a list of every single writing goal you have.

Then look at your list and pick the *one goal* that makes your heart sing the most; the one you absolutely have to write before the new year is out.

Take a separate piece of paper.

Write your number one goal - *and this goal alone* - upon it.

Welcome to your new year's writing resolution.

Take the piece of paper with your list of other writing goals.

Fold it up.

Put it away in a drawer where it won't distract you.

For the whole of January do nothing but focus on your number one writing goal.

Repeat for February.

And repeat as necessary, until this goal is achieved.

Know that your other writing goals are still important.

You haven't abandoned them.

They're simply waiting in that drawer for a time when they will have your undivided attention.

And they will get your undivided attention, once you've finished the piece of writing that is most important to you.

Then you can go back to your list and pick a new number one to focus on.

When it comes to your writing resolutions, **prioritising = clarity**.

And **clarity = success**.

*Side note: I ran a weekly writing workshop in London for six years. A lovely and very talented writer used to come to the workshop, always brimming with ideas. Each week he'd read something different - the latest chapter from his novel-in-progress, the latest story from his anthology-in-progress, the latest poem from his collection-in-progress. Then, one week, he asked me why he never seemed to get anything finished. I told him to pick one of his projects and focus on nothing else until it was done. That year, he finally completed his novel and published a collection of poems. **Focus gets things finished.***

How to Write a Book in a Month* – Without Losing the Plot

(*OK, so when I say 'book' I mean first draft and when I say 'month' I mean 4 - 6 weeks)

I've been writing books for fifteen years now and whenever I'm asked how long it takes to write a novel, I always reply, 'around nine months'. Usually followed by some naff quip about the length of time it takes to make a baby.

But sometimes I've had to write books to a much shorter deadline and I've discovered that not only is it possible to write a first draft in four to six weeks, it can actually be strangely enjoyable.

So, if you're a novelist who has always told yourself that it takes months / years to write a book...

Or a self-publishing author who needs to up your output...

Or you're thinking of doing *NaNoWriMo* (a crazy online initiative where people attempt to write a novel in a month)...

... here are my tips for writing a first draft in four to six weeks without totally losing the plot.

1. Know where you're going before you start

If you're going to write crazy fast you need to know where you're going - and with who. So sketch out a rough outline of the plot and characters before you begin. These can obviously change as you get further into the story but to get off to a flying start, you need to be headed in the right direction - and be very clear on what that direction should be.

2. Divvy up your word count

Divide your total word count into weekly word counts. Then divide your weekly word counts into daily word counts. 2,600 words in a day (allowing for weekends off) sounds infinitely more achievable than 80,000 words in six weeks. Stick to this schedule and you should avoid a one-way ticket to Crazy Town.

3. Allow yourself to get 'messy'

I would give this advice to any writer, regardless of deadline, but it is ultra-important when you only have six weeks. You don't have the time to be overly-critical, so give your inner editor some time off and JUST WRITE.

4. Write fast

Er, yeah, seems obvious I know, but what I mean is, don't pause for hours to ponder exactly the right word. If it doesn't come straight away, use a holding word - or if you can't think of a holding word just write 'xxxxx' and come back to it later. You have to stay in the flow and the flow cannot be slow.

5. Start a new writing day by editing the previous day's work

This helps you get back into the flow of the story and frees you up to write messily - when you know you'll be coming back to make improvements the next day.

6. Get physical

It's vital for your health and sanity to make sure you're still getting plenty of fresh air and exercise during your writing marathon. I find regular walks, runs and yoga workouts to be life savers. Especially if you do hit a block with your writing.

Getting outside really helps to clear any creative cobwebs. If for whatever reason, you can't get outside, then get up and dance like a loony around your living room for ten minutes. Sometimes blocked ideas literally need to be shaken free. (Don't overdo the physical exercise though - view it as something to invigorate, not exhaust you.)

7. Have at least one day off a week

And make this day off away from your computer. Away from your house if at all possible. Fear and pressure can make us want to chain ourselves to our laptops till the darn thing's finished but this is actually massively counter-productive. Getting away from your work in progress and having some F.U.N. can work wonders for stimulating your writing flow.

8. Eat healthily and drink lemon water by the gallon

The fact is, you are embarking upon a writing marathon. You need to make sure your brain and those poor keyboard-bashing fingers are getting the proper fuel. Eat fresh food. And by that I mean, fresh fruit and veg - not freshly delivered pizza. And drink loads of water - with lemon juice for some added zing and vit C. I know writers are supposed to be tortured alcoholics, slumped over their typewriters, necking Jack Daniels and chaining Marlborough Reds, but if you've only got a month to write a book, you haven't got time for hangovers. Or deleting your way through the sozzled, sorry prose of the night before.

9. Sleep. Sleep. Sleep

To write quickly and well, you need to be at your sharpest and to be at your sharpest, you need to stock up on your supply of sleep. And *good quality* sleep now we come to mention it.
So try to avoid having a final surf of the net when you get into bed and falling down a late night Facebook / twitter hole.

Unwind by having a warm bath or watching a good movie. Switch off fully from your work in progress until the next day's writing. Give your work a chance to percolate and give yourself a chance to rest and recharge.

10. Have fun with it

The notion of having fun when you're up against a crazy writing deadline might seem totally insane but you'd be amazed at how much you can get done when you take the pressure off yourself and decide to just enjoy the experience. This has been the biggest revelation to me - how much I enjoy writing a super-speedy first draft.

The first drafts I've written in four to six weeks have been some of the most focused and creative experiences of my life. I feel totally immersed in the world of the book, without any of the usual pain in the butt niggles of writer's block and indecision and self-doubt - I just don't have the time for them!

Let Your Creative Passions Lead You Back to You

It had been billed to me as (and I quote) 'a holiday club for troubled teens', and I had been asked to run a drama workshop every day for the week.

I knew as soon as the first chair went flying that my carefully prepared programme of fun drama exercises (*'hey guys, let's all pretend to be trees'*) was not going to cut it with this crowd.

These teens weren't just 'troubled' by not having the latest x-box game or designer trainers, they were troubled by things like abject poverty, damp-infested homes on crime-riddled council estates and being pushed from pillar to post in foster care.

The last thing they needed was some well-meaning eejit telling them to pretend to be a sycamore.

So, as I broke up the fight and prayed to the God of Drama Workshops for salvation, I mentally binned my week's programme and started again.

'This week, you're all going to create and perform in your own play,' I yelled over the noise.

'What, we get to write the play?' a sullen-faced girl asked in between gum-chews.

'Yep,' I replied, wondering if I'd just made the biggest mistake of my professional life.

'And it can be about anything we like?'

'Yep.'

Silence.

Followed by an explosion of chatter.

But this time it wasn't about who was going to kill who, it was about their play.

And the sullen-faced girl, who had been instrumental in inciting the chair-throwing, was transformed.

Her eyes shone, her arms windmilled wildly as ideas burst from her.

'We could do ….'

'Or how about…?'

'Wouldn't it be cool if…?'

Her enthusiasm was infectious and soon the whole group had united behind the bones of an idea – about a group of kids who find the courage to stand up to the drug dealer on their estate.

All I had to do was hover in the background, offering suggestions and help when it was needed.

By the end of day one they'd created the basic outline of their plot.

At the start of day two, they all raced into the room, along with a few extras who'd heard about the 'drug dealer play' and wanted to swap from the workshops they were on to be a part of it.

I watched and guided as the girl once again took charge of the group, her passion for drama lighting up the room.

By Wednesday the play was written and cast.

By Thursday it had been workshopped and rehearsed.

And on Friday, *'Dirty Dealings'* was performed in an impromptu showcase to all of the other kids, their parents and carers and the holiday club staff.

All the cast shone but the transformation in that one girl was incredible.

And the lesson lodged deep inside of me: our passions always lead us back to our true selves, no matter what crap we might be dealing with.

When she'd first arrived at the workshop, the girl hadn't just created a mask, she'd created an entire exclusion zone of anger around her. But as soon as she was allowed to plug into her passion for drama, her guard lowered and we all saw the exuberant, fun-loving girl she really was at heart.

I found out later that the girl had come to the UK from Eastern Europe as the very young child of asylum seeker parents and she'd been living in a children's home for several years.

I've often thought about her in the years since that workshop, wondering what happened to her and hoping that our week together sparked something inside of her, a way out from her problems; a way back to her true self.

And I continue to use my encounter with her as inspiration. My first young adult novel, *Dear Dylan* was loosely based on her and in *True Face* I have a whole section on the importance of identifying and pursuing your passions.

Her zest for drama, in spite of the battles she was facing on a daily basis, left an indelible mark upon me.

And this is the most important thing about pursuing our passions: when we do so, we shine so brightly we light the way for others to pursue their passions too.

So, if you're feeling a little battered down by life, if you know fear of being hurt is causing you to put on a mask or even create an exclusion zone of anger, hurt or indifference, ask yourself these two simple questions:

What are my passions?

How can I spend one hour today in the pursuit of one of them?

Let your creative passions lead you back to you...

Dear Dare to Dream: Should I Self-Publish My Novel?

Dear Dare to Dream,

I feel a bit like I've lost my mojo.

This year, I started sending the first three chapters of a novel I've written out to literary agents. Three of them asked to see the whole thing but then never got back to me, not even to say no.

I've worked on this book for four years and I feel it's good enough to be published, but I am now losing my confidence and I worry that if I self-publish I will make a fool of myself. Basically, I feel like a crap writer.

A writer friend of mine is dead against me self-publishing, telling me that I'm good enough to get a book deal, but I just don't know and I'm such a hands-on type person. It hurts sitting around doing nothing.

I've started working on another novel but it feels as if I'm just building sandcastles. I want to have something published to give me the confidence and power to write.

Have you ever felt this way? So down in the dumps?

And should I take the bull by the horns and just self-publish, even if so many tell me that it's 'vanity publishing'? I know it sounds silly but I can just see my colleagues sniggering behind my back and saying, 'she thinks she can write!' Stupid, I know.

I guess I just need some encouragement, or just to know that others have felt this way too...

Down in the Dumps x

Dear Down in the Dumps,

Once upon a time, writing made me so sad, I sat in the corner of my kitchen floor and cried.

I cried so long and so hard, I forgot I had a chocolate cake baking and it burned to a cinder.

Normally, *nothing* makes me forget I have a cake baking, so yes, writing has definitely made me as down in the dumps as you are feeling right now.

But I wasn't crying because I couldn't get a book deal. I was crying because I'd got a book deal, had three novels published, and then been dropped by my publisher.

And the reason I felt so cake-burningly bad was because it truly felt as if my life was over.

And it truly felt as if my life was over because getting a book deal had meant so, so much to me.

It had made me feel good about myself for the first time in years.

It had made me feel as if I'd finally achieved something in my work life.

It had given me the confidence to leave a relationship that had been destroying me from the inside out.

It had made me believe that I was finally a writer.

*I wasn't a university drop-out any more - **I was a writer**.*

*I wasn't a loser in love any more - **I was a writer**.*

*I wasn't worthless any more - **I was a writer**.*

I thought that losing my book deal meant that I was no longer a writer. Just as you think that not getting a book deal makes you a 'crappy writer'.

But I was wrong.

And so are you.

Having a book deal does not make you a writer.

Writing makes you a writer.

Writing even when you're bone-tired and emotionally drained.

Writing around the edges of your busy life because you'd rather do it then than not at all.

Because you can't do it 'not at all'.

Because the words and the stories and the characters and the feelings are just bursting to come out.

And they all want to burst out through you and your own unique voice.

So, dear Down in the Dumps, you have a choice.

You can either let a bunch of strangers who can't even be bothered to reply to you determine your fate, or you can take full control of your writing destiny.

That's what I did, when I lost my book deal.

After crying and burning a cake and throwing a pity party for about a month, I picked myself up and I found my way back to the beginning. Back to the time when I wrote purely for the love of it.

And I wrote a novel, purely for the love of it and I self-published it so that I could give it away for free, purely for the love of it.

About a month after the book came out, I was invited to speak on a panel at London Book Fair.

My fellow panellists were two best-selling authors, a very well-known literary agent and the head of a major publishing house. I was invited along as the token self-publisher.

During the course of our debate I was roundly sneered at and put down by my fellow panellists - to the point where one member of the audience walked out in disgust.

There would have been a time when this would have really upset me, especially when one of the novelists suggested that the book I'd self-published was probably crap.

But if anything, her sneering only got me more fired up. Because I wasn't writing to massage my ego or for money or fame, *I was doing it for the love of it*. And I might not have been a best-selling novelist with a book deal, but at least I wasn't a self-important arsehole.

My self-published novel went on to win a national book award and I now have book deals with eight different publishers, in three different countries. But I'm also building my own indie imprint where I can enjoy complete creative control over my writing career.

I'm proof positive of the incredible things that can happen to writers when they take their careers into their own hands.

But don't just take my word for it, pay a visit to *The Creative Penn*, a fantastic website run by indie author, Joanna Penn. It's crammed full of inspirational interviews with writers who are achieving phenomenal success without a traditional book deal.

And it also contains loads of helpful tips and advice for writers who want to achieve the same.

I also recommend you read *Turning Pro* by Steven Pressfield. It's a kick up the butt in book form.

The only people who sneer at self-publishing and call it 'vanity' publishing these days are old-school, self-important, literary snobs or unhappy people too fearful to chase their own dreams.

I'm sure your writer friend has your best interests at heart, but self-publishing isn't a sign of failure - it's a sign of enterprise and passion. It's the sign of a true writer who doesn't want to let anything hold them back.

If a musician builds a following on YouTube prior to getting a record deal they aren't laughed at or called stupid. Just ask Jessie J or the Arctic Monkeys or Lily Allen.

So, why not follow their example?

Get your book out there.

Get writing the next one.

Get back to the beginning and write and publish for the love of it. Nothing else.

You aren't building sandcastles, you're building imaginary worlds for others to enjoy.

And you're building a happier future for yourself by daring to dream.

As Ray Bradbury so eloquently puts it:

"To sum it all up, if you want to write, if you want to create, you must be the most sublime fool that God ever turned out and sent rambling. You must write every single day of your life. You must read dreadful dumb books and glorious books, and let them wrestle in beautiful fights inside your head, vulgar one moment, brilliant the next. You must lurk in libraries and climb the stacks like ladders to sniff books like perfumes and wear books like hats upon your crazy heads. I wish you a wrestling match with your Creative Muse that will last a lifetime. I wish craziness and foolishness and madness upon you. May you live with hysteria, and out of it make fine stories — science fiction or otherwise. Which finally means, may you be in love every day for the next 20,000 days. And out of that love, remake a world."

Wishing you much love and writing happiness,

Siobhan x

And finally...

I hope you've enjoyed reading my musings and that they've inspired you to dare to love, create and dream.

If you have enjoyed *Dare to Dream*, I'd really appreciate it if you could take a moment to give it a star-rating on Amazon or Goodreads and to recommend it to your friends. As I'm publishing it myself I only have a marketing budget of about £2.50, so some good ol' word-of-mouth would be wonderful.

£1 from every copy of this book sold is being donated to the charity Leuka to help fund a cure for leukaemia. Thank you so much for buying this book and donating to such a great and much-needed cause.

For more of the same, or to find out more about working with me, or to be featured in *Dear Dare to Dream*, please come on over to the *Dare to Dream* blog at:

www.daretodreamcoaching.co.uk

Love and blessings,

Siobhan x

Acknowledgements

Thank you so much to all of the readers of the *Dare to Dream* blog who've taken the time to contact me over the past couple of years. Your messages of support mean the world to me and have turned blogging from a solitary pursuit into a real sense of community.

Thank you to Michael A. Hill for the beautiful cover. To anyone in search of a book cover designer, I can't recommend Michael highly enough.

Huge thanks to all of my wonderful friends and family. Re-reading and editing the posts for this book have reminded me yet again of how blessed I am to have you in my life.

And thank you to YOU for buying this book – and thereby donating £1 to the charity Leuka, helping find a cure for leukaemia.

True Face

Siobhan Curham (Faber & Faber, April 2015)

It's time to unmask the real you.

From body image, bullying and social media to love, sex and more, Siobhan Curham helps women and girls to be honest, dream big and create lives that are happy and fulfilling in this empowering and inspirational book.

We are living in the age of the image – the perfect image. From the constant bombardment of air-brushed photos, to the dubious lifestyle choices promoted by celebrities and the goldfish bowl of social media, women are under pressure as never before to project a persona of perfection. And this is having a catastrophic effect, with girls as young as seven developing eating disorders.

True Face is part mystery, part adventure. The mystery comes in working out who you truly are, the adventure comes in planning the life you really want to lead.

'An important and inspirational book.' **The Bookseller**

'A rousing and informative read.' **Mumsnet**

'Curham is a lovely writer, who can make the obvious feel fresh and negative seem manageable.' **The Debrief**

'This book is so significant … it made me realise that I was doing things I didn't realise and it's empowered me a lot from a simple read.' **To Another World**

'A great piece of literary inspiration in a world that is often filled with fake voices that can cloud your judgement.' **Sister Spooky**

'It feels like you have a wise sister talking to you … *True Face* is inspirational.' **Luna's Little Library**

'A brilliant concept … I felt like a more confident, more honest version of myself once I'd finished.' **Teen Book Hoots**

'I felt much more inspired after finishing *True Face*. So much so that I stopped to write a letter to myself, reminding myself of how far I've come, despite the obstacles that have been in my way.' **Chrissi Reads**

'Offers some really good tips and advice for helping you come to terms with who you are and get to grips with the issues that affect you … A great book.' **The Big Book Project**